Creating a Self-Tuning Oracle Database

Automating Oracle9i Dynamic SGA Performance

Donald K. Burleson

This book is dedicated to the memory of Amos Lavender.

Creating a Self-Tuning Oracle Database - Automating Oracle9i Dynamic SGA Performance

By Donald K. Burleson

Printed in the United States of America.

Published in Kittrell, North Carolina, USA.

Oracle In-Focus Series: Book #3

Series Editor: Don Burleson

Editors: Robert Strickland, Janet Burleson, John Lavender, and Linda Webb

Production Editor: Teri Wade

Cover Design: Bryan Hoff

Printing History:

February 2003 for First Edition

ISBN: 0-9727513-2-7

Library of Congress Control Number: 2003090827

Table of Contents

Using the Online Code Depot

Your purchase of this book provides you with complete access to the online code depot.

All of the scripts in this book are located at the following URL:

www.rampant.cc/st.htm

All of the code scripts in this book can be downloaded in a zip format, ready to load and use on your database.

Throughout the text, scripts in the code depot are named and called-out in a box like this:

myscript.sql

Once you have downloaded the code, you should easily be able to locate and run your scripts.

If you need technical assistance in downloading or accessing the scripts, please contact Rampant TechPress at info@rampant.cc.

Conventions Used in This Book

It is critical for any technical publication to follow rigorous standards and employ consistent punctuation conventions to make the text easy to read.

However, this is not an easy task. Within Oracle, there are many types of notations that can confuse a reader. Some Oracle utilities such as STATSPACK and TKPROF are always spelled with CAPITAL letters, while Oracle parameters and procedures have varying naming conventions in the Oracle documentation. It is also important to remember that many Oracle commands are case sensitive, and are always left in their original executable form, and never altered with italics or capitalization.

Hence, all Rampant TechPress books follow these conventions:

- **Parameters** - All Oracle parameters will be *lowercase italics*. Exceptions to this rule are parameter arguments that are commonly capitalized (KEEP pool, TKPROF), these will be left in ALL CAPS.

- **Variables** – All PL/SQL program variables and arguments will also remain in lowercase italics (*dbms_job, dbms_utility*).

- **Tables & dictionary objects** – All data dictionary objects are referenced in lowercase italics (*dba_indexes, v$sql*). This includes all *v$* and *x$* views *(x$kcbcbh, v$parameter)* and dictionary views *(dba_tables, user_indexes).*

- **SQL** – All SQL is formatted for easy use in the code depot, and all SQL is displayed in lowercase. The main SQL terms (select, from, where, group by, order by, having) will always appear on a separate line.

- **Program names** – Programs and code depot script names are always in *lowercase italics.*

- **Products** – All products that are known to the author are capitalized according to the vendor specifications (IBM, DBXray, etc). All names known by Rampant TechPress to be trademark names appear in this text as initial caps. References to UNIX are always made in uppercase.

Acknowledgements

This type of highly technical reference book requires the dedicated efforts of many people. Even though we are the authors, our work ends when we deliver the content. After each chapter is delivered, several Oracle DBAs carefully review and correct the technical content. After the technical review, experienced copy editors polish the grammar and syntax. The finished work is then reviewed as page proofs and turned over to the production manager, who arranges the creation of the online code depot and manages the cover art, printing distribution, and warehousing.

In short, the authors play a small role in the development of this book, and we need to thank and acknowledge everyone who helped bring this book to fruition:

- **John Lavender**, for the production management, including the coordination of the cover art, page proofing, printing, and distribution.

- **Robert Strickland,** for his excellent copyediting and format checking services.

- **Teri Wade,** for her help in the production of the page proofs.

- **Bryan Hoff**, for his exceptional cover design and graphics.

- **Janet Burleson**, for her assistance with the web site, and for creating the code depot and the online shopping cart for this book.

- **Linda Webb**, for her expert page-proofing services.

- **Mike Ault**, for his expert technical review of the content.

With my sincerest thanks,

Donald K. Burleson

Donald K. Burleson

Preface

The advent of Oracle9i provides a mechanism for the automation of Oracle SGA tuning. Because almost every Oracle parameter can now be changed with an *"alter system"* command, the Oracle professional now has the ability to dynamically change all areas of the Oracle System Global Area (SGA).

This exciting new feature lays the foundation for creating a self-tuning Oracle database. It is imperative that the Oracle professional understand the tools and techniques that are used to monitor and adjust the size of the SGA RAM regions within the Oracle instance.

This book is intended to get you started in creating your own self-tuning architecture and shows some of the common techniques used to monitor and automatically change the configuration of Oracle in response to anticipated changes in processing.

This text is targeted at senior Oracle professionals who already have substantial knowledge of the internal mechanisms for changing the configuration of Oracle. However, we have tried to place lots of illustrative examples throughout the text and show how you can design a simple self-tuning mechanism.

While the scope of performance tuning is too broad for this small text, we show actual examples of working code and demonstrate how you can easily build mechanisms to self-tune your Oracle database.

Chapter 1

Overview of the Oracle9i SGA Regions

When an Oracle database is started, the Oracle executable issues the *malloc( )* command to create a region of RAM memory. The SGA is commonly called the Oracle region because it is a region of RAM memory on the database server RAM heap.

The Oracle DBA controls the size of the SGA, and proper SGA management can have a huge impact on performance. However, we must remember that the SGA is a static memory region, and the needs of the Oracle database are constantly changing. Until Oracle9i, the SGA was not dynamic and could not be altered. After Oracle9i became commonplace in 2002, the dynamic adjustment of the SGA was common, and there is also speculation that a future release of Oracle will reconfigure itself based on the needs of the database.

However, until then, changing the SGA requires constant monitoring, and it is sometimes a good approach to develop a general setting for the SGA parameters based on the historical needs of the application.

RAM Allocation at Oracle Instance Startup

To fully understand RAM usage, it is interesting to observe Oracle RAM and CPU allocation at startup time.

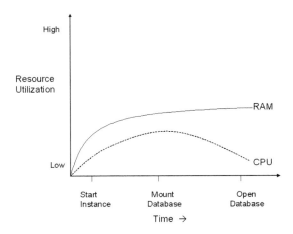

Figure 1.1 – The startup signature for an Oracle instance

Figure 1.1 is a time-based snapshot of an Oracle database's CPU and RAM resource consumption at database startup time. We see the RAM allocated when the SGA is started and the RAM usage remains relatively constant after this point. As for CPU usage, we see that the CPU stress peaks during database mounting and declines as the background processes become idle.

It is important to know that the allocation of RAM memory for an Oracle server can be done solely with mathematics, and no expensive performance monitors are required to properly estimate the initial RAM demands of your Oracle database. Once your Oracle database is configured, you can change the RAM according to demand.

Prior to release 8.1.7, the most difficult part of Oracle RAM optimization in any environment was accurately predicting the high water mark of dedicated, connected user sessions once the instance was started. This was because of a bug in the *v$resource_limit* view. After release

Creating a Self-Tuning Oracle Database

8.1.7, you can use *v$resource_limit* to see the high water mark of connected sessions since startup time.

If we have an unexpected spike of dedicated, connected sessions, it is possible that we would exceed the amount of RAM on the server, causing active programs' RAM regions to go out to the swap disk. In sum, the goal is to fully allocate RAM without ever experiencing RAM paging and to re-allocate RAM within the Oracle SGA to optimize performance.

To see the size of your SGA, you can issue the *show sga* command from SQL*Plus, as shown below. The output of the *show sga* command appears here:

```
SQL> connect system/manager as sysdba;

SQL> show sga

Total System Global Area        405323864 bytes
Fixed Size                          49240 bytes
Variable Size                   354066432 bytes
Database Buffers                 49152000 bytes
Redo Buffers                      2056192 bytes
```

Now, let's take a quick look at the important regions within the SGA. The most important areas of RAM within the SGA include:

- **Data Buffer Caches** – These RAM areas define RAM space for incoming data blocks and are governed by the following parameters. The sum of all of these parameter values determines the total space reserved for Oracle data blocks.

  - *db_cache_size*
  - *db_keep_cache_size)*

- *db_recycle_cache_size*
- *db_2k_cache_size*
- *db_4k_cache_size*
- *db_8k_cache_size*
- *db_16k_cache_size*
- *db_32k_cache_size*

- **Log Buffer** – This is the RAM space for writing redo log files. The *log_buffer* parameter should never exceed 5 megabytes, and this RAM space is used solely to hold the redo images until the LGWR background process writes the redo log entries into the redo log filesystem.

- **Shared Pool** - This RAM area is used to process SQL statements (inside a shared pool area called the library cache) and hold control structures for the instance. It is governed by the *shared_pool_size* parameter.

To re-allocate RAM within Oracle, we use *alter system* commands to change important Oracle parameters that govern the size of the memory regions within the SGA. Let's take a close look at these parameters and see how they are used.

Oracle SGA Parameters

Self-tuning Oracle's memory regions involves altering the values of a number of Oracle parameters. While there are over 250 Oracle9i parameters that govern the configuration of every aspect of the database, there are only a handful of

Oracle9i parameters that are important for Oracle SGA tuning:

- **db_cache_size** - This parameter determines the number of database block buffers in the Oracle SGA and is the single most important parameter in Oracle memory.

- **db_keep_cache_size** - *db_keep_cache_size* is used to store small tables that perform full table scans. This data buffer pool was a sub-pool of *db_block_buffers* in Oracle8i.

- **db_recycle_cache_size** - This is reserved for table blocks from very large tables that perform full table scans. This was *buffer_pool_keep* in Oracle8i.

- **large_pool_size** - This is a special area of the shared pool that is reserved for SGA usage when using the multi-threaded server. The large pool is used for parallel query and RMAN processing, as well as setting the size of the Java pool.

- **log_buffer** - This parameter determines the amount of memory to allocate for Oracle's redo log buffers. If there is a high amount of update activity, the *log_buffer* should be allocated more space.

- **shared_pool_size** - This parameter defines the pool that is shared by all users in the system, including SQL areas and data dictionary caching. A large *shared_pool_size* is not always better than a smaller shared pool. If your application contains nonreusable SQL, you may get better performance with a smaller shared pool.

- ***sort_area_size*** - This parameter determines the memory region that is allocated for in-memory sorting. When the *stats$sysstat* value sorts (disk) becomes excessive, you may want to allocate additional memory.

- ***hash_area_size*** - This parameter determines the memory region reserved for hash joins. Starting with Oracle9i, Oracle Corporation does not recommend using *hash_area_size* unless the instance is configured with the shared server option. Oracle recommends that you enable automatic sizing of SQL work areas by setting *pga_aggregate_target*. *hash_area_size* is retained only for backward compatibility purposes.

- ***pga_aggregate_target*** – This parameter defines the RAM area reserved for system-wide sorting and hash joins.

- ***sga_max_size*** – This parameter defines the maximum size of the Oracle SGA, and cannot be modified while the instance is running.

With over 250 Oracle parameters and thousands of metrics, it is no small task for the Oracle administrator to zero-in on the most important measures of the health of his or her Oracle database. Many database administrators use the following list to get a general idea of the overall health of their systems.

- **Data Buffer Hit Ratio Alert** - This report alerts the DBA when the data buffer hit ratio falls below the preset threshold.

- **Redo Log Space Requests Alert** - If redo log space requests are greater than 0, you may want to increase the *log_buffer* parameter.

- **Shared Pool Contention Alert** - Enqueue deadlocks can indicate contention within the shared pool, as well as locking-related problems.

- **System Waits Alert** - This query interrogates the Oracle event structures to locate events that may be experiencing excessive waits. If you experience waits on latch free, enqueue, LGWR waits, or buffer busy waits, you need to locate the cause of the contention.

- **Library Cache Misses Alert** - This query looks for excessive library cache miss ratios. When the library cache miss ratio is greater than .02, you may want to increase the value of the *shared_pool_size* parameter.

- **Database Writer Contention Alert** - This query checks Oracle for values in summed dirty queue length, write requests, and DBWR checkpoints. When the write request length is greater than 3 or your DBWR checkpoint waits, you need to look at tuning the database writer processes.

- **Data Dictionary Miss Ratio Alert** - This script alerts the DBA when requests for data dictionary metadata are high. Increasing the *shared_pool_size* parameter can sometimes relieve this problem.

- **Data Dictionary Object Alert** - This report can reveal internal contention within the Oracle data dictionary, as well as a high rate of requests for dictionary metadata.

For more information on these alerts, see http://www.remote-dba.net. Next, let's take a brief tour of the important SGA RAM areas and see why they are important for building a self-tuning Oracle9i database.

The Data Buffer Caches

Oracle9i allows the SGA to include up to seven RAM regions for caching incoming disk data blocks. They are the KEEP pool, RECYCLE pool, and DEFAULT pool, plus instantiated pools for 2K, 4K, 8K, 16K, and 32K data blocks (Figure 1.2).

Please note that the KEEP and RECYCLE regions were subsets of the DEFAULT pool prior to Oracle9i, but are separate RAM regions in Oracle9i and beyond. Remember, once one of the sized pools (2K-32K) is assigned to the DEFAULT pool, its size cannot be assigned to another buffer. The sized data buffers correspond to tablespaces, and a 32K block tablespace will load into the 32K data buffer.

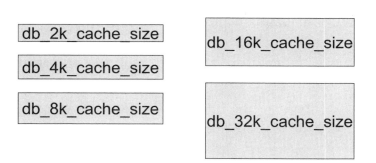

Figure 1.2 – The RAM data buffer caches

Prior to Oracle9i, the KEEP and RECYCLE pools were a sub-set of the DEFAULT pool. The DEFAULT pool is created by the *db_cache_size* parameter in Oracle9i, while former versions use the *db_block_buffers* parameter. Starting with Oracle9i, the KEEP and RECYCLE pools are allocated, in addition to the *db_cache_size*. Also, note that Oracle9i allows the use of multiple block regions, ranging in size from 2K-32K, each with its own distinct buffer cache.

The buffer caches are in memory areas of the SGA where incoming Oracle data blocks are kept. These data buffer sizes can have a tremendous impact on overall system performance. There is a greater probability that data from past transactions will still be in a large buffer, minimizing expensive physical disk I/O in Oracle. RAM access is at least two thousand times faster than disk access.

The Log Buffer

Oracle creates redo logs for all update operations. In case of disk failure, the redo logs are used to roll forward, since they contain the after image of all row changes.

First, the after images are written to the log buffer area of RAM. The LGWR background process then transfers the images to Oracle online redo log files. In the last step, the ARCH background process writes the online redo log files to the archived redo log file system, where they are available to recover the database in the event of disk failure.

However, some shops avoid this overhead by using triple-mirrored disks and running their databases in NOARCHIVELOG mode. These shops believe the high redundancy is sufficient protection from a disk crash, and they deliberately reject the ability to roll the database forward, in return for faster performance.

The Shared Pool

The shared pool is the most important area of the SGA, except for the data buffer caches. There are a number of sub-areas within the SGA, each with its own important purpose. Unfortunately, all of the sub-areas are controlled by the single *shared_pool_size* parameter.

Since it is not possible to dedicate separate regions of memory for the shared pool components, the shared pool is usually the second-largest SGA memory area depending on the size of the *db_cache_size* parameter. The shared pool contains RAM memory regions that serve the following purposes:

- **Library cache** – The library cache contains the current SQL execution plan information. It also holds stored procedures and trigger code.

- **Dictionary cache** - The dictionary cache stores environmental information, which includes referential integrity, table definitions, indexing information, and other metadata stored within Oracle's internal tables.

- **Session information** – Systems that use SQL*Net version 2 with a multi-threaded server need this area to store session information. Beginning with Oracle9i, the *v$session* view contains information related to Oracle*Net users.

RAM and the Oracle Server

The purpose of server optimization for the Oracle database is to manage the RAM and CPU resources of the machine and ensure that expensive RAM is not under-utilized. The techniques used to optimize Oracle database performance on large UNIX platforms are similar to those used for a MS-Windows system.

Most Oracle consultants see shops waste millions of dollars worth of RAM. The RAM is under-allocated because the DBA is unaware of how to accurately analyze the RAM demands of the database. RAM is very expensive on larger servers and depreciates regardless of use.

The knowledgeable DBA will know how to accurately predict the maximum RAM demands for the database and will allocate RAM fully, holding in reserve only enough to accommodate user connection spikes. Let's review disk swapping and see how this is accomplished.

RAM and Swap Disk

Whatever the operating platform, the processing demands of the Oracle database must not exceed the real RAM memory of the server. All large servers share RAM resources through a Virtual Memory (VM) scheme. Oracle servers (Windows, UNIX, and OS-390) manage excessive RAM demands with a special swap disk, and virtual memory exploits the fact that not every executing task is constantly referencing its RAM memory region.

Since some RAM regions are accessed intermittently, vendors have developed paging algorithms that shift these memory pages to the swap disk when they are not in use.

The *swap disk* is a special disk area that provides for RAM sharing, primarily by storing page frames of inactive disk programs. The least-frequently-used (LRU) RAM pages are offloaded so that new applications can simultaneously share the same memory. After inactive RAM frames are paged-out to the disk, the operating system can utilize the freed memory for other active tasks.

If the inactive program later resumes execution, the RAM frames are paged-in from the swap disk.

This reloading of RAM pages from one memory area to another is called swapping. Swapping is very time-consuming and degrades performance of the application.

The swap disk allows simultaneous RAM usage greater than the real amount of RAM, but performance will be seriously compromised if the swap disk is used for active programs. The impaired performance is due to the much slower read times from the swap disk, compared to RAM. Disk access is measured in milliseconds, or millionths of a second, while RAM access is measured in nanoseconds, or billionths of a second.

Not all of this difference can be practically realized because of Oracle overhead, but most experts say that Oracle RAM is about 2,500 times faster than disk access.

In a Virtual Memory configuration, the OS writes RAM to the swap disk before the real RAM is exceeded, anticipating a memory shortage. This way, the LRU frames will already be on the swap disk in the event of a real RAM shortage.

The goal for an Oracle server is to keep the RAM memory demands of the database and database connections below the amount of physical RAM memory. We can control the amount of RAM used by the database SGA in an Oracle environment by issuing *alter system* commands. These commands can increase or decrease RAM memory as needed.

The allocated size of the SGA is displayed at startup in the Oracle alert log, and also on the console as shown below.

```
SQL> startup

ORACLE instance started.

Total System Global Area   143421172 bytes
Fixed Size                    282356 bytes
Variable Size              117440512 bytes
Database Buffers            25165824 bytes
Redo Buffers                  532480 bytes
Database mounted.
Database opened.
```

The *show sga* command also displays the SGA RAM region. The total SGA size is 143 megabytes in the example below.

```
SQL> connect system/manager as sysdba

Connected.

SQL> show sga

Total System Global Area   143421172 bytes
Fixed Size                    282356 bytes
Variable Size              117440512 bytes
Database Buffers            25165824 bytes
Redo Buffers                  532480 bytes
```

We'll see next how to quickly find the amount of RAM on the server.

Determining the RAM on your Oracle Server

Most Oracle servers will show you the amount of RAM with just a few simple commands. Specific commands are required to display the RAM usage for each UNIX dialect. (Table 1.1)

Dialect of UNIX	RAM display command
HP/UX	swapinfo –tm
Solaris	prtconf | grep -i mem
AIX	lsdev -C | grep mem
DEC-UNIX	uerf -r 300 | grep -i mem
Linux	free

Table 1.1 – Summary of RAM memory commands

RAM on IBM-AIX UNIX

The AIX dialect requires a two-step command to display the amount of available RAM. First, the *lsdev* command shows the devices that are attached to the UNIX server. This large listing of all devices can be reduced to show only the RAM devices by sending its output to the *grep* command:

```
root> lsdev -C|grep mem

mem0        Available 00-00            Memory
```

The display indicates that *mem0* is the name of the memory device on this AIX server. To find the amount of memory on this AIX server, the *lsattr-El* command (which passes *mem0* as an argument) is issued. The new display indicates that the server has 2 gigabytes of RAM memory attached to the *mem0* device, as shown below:

```
root> lsattr -El mem0

size     2048 Total amount of physical memory in Mbytes  False
goodsize 2048 Amount of usable physical memory in Mbytes False
```

RAM in Linux

Displaying the amount of RAM on the server is even easier in Linux. Use the *free* command to quickly obtain the following information:

```
root> free
              total      used      free    shared   buffers    cached
Mem:        3728668    504688   3223980     41316    430072     29440
-/+ buffers/cache:       45176   3683492
Swap:        265032       608    264424
```

RAM on MS-Windows

On the MS-Windows server, the amount of RAM is displayed by going to Start → Settings →Control Panel →

System and then clicking on the "General" tab (Figure 1.3). The server below has 1,250 megabytes of RAM.

Figure 1.3 – The MS-windows system display screen

Once the size of the MS-Windows RAM and SGA is known, it is time to consider the RAM usage for Oracle connections.

Reserving RAM for Database Connections

Oracle allocates an OS area of RAM for every connected user if the system uses external PGA regions (i.e. if the *pga_aggregate_target* parameter is not used and you are not using the multi-threaded server). To determine the optimal RAM allocation for any Oracle server, the DBA may use a formula. We will assume in this example that the server is a dedicated MS-Windows Oracle server, and that Oracle is the only program running on the server.

For dedicated Oracle servers, the maximum total RAM is computed as follows:

- **OS Reserved RAM** – This is RAM required to run the OS kernel and system functions.

  > 20% of total RAM for MS-Windows
  > 10% of total RAM for UNIX

- **Oracle Database Connections RAM** – Each Oracle connection requires OS RAM regions for sorting and hash joins. (This does not apply when using the Oracle multi-threaded server or *pga_aggregate_target.*) The maximum amount of RAM required for a session is as follows:

  > 2 megabytes RAM session overhead
  > + *sort_area_size*
  > + *hash_area_size*

- **Oracle SGA RAM** – This is determined by the Oracle parameter settings. The total is easily found by either the *show sga* command or the value of the *sga_memory_max* parameter.

We should subtract 20 percent from the total available RAM to allow for MS-Windows overhead. Windows uses RAM resources even when idle, and the 20 percent deduction is necessary to get the real free RAM on an idle server. Once the amount of RAM on the server is known, we will be in a position to size the Oracle database for RAM usage.

First, we need to know the high water mark (HWM) of Oracle connections. As noted previously, each session connected to the Windows server requires a memory region for the program global area (PGA), unless Oracle's multi-threaded server architecture or *pga_aggregate_target* is utilized.

The high water mark of connected Oracle sessions can be determined in several ways. One popular method uses Oracle login and logoff system-level triggers to record sessions in a statistics table. Another method uses Oracle STATSPACK to display the values from the *stats$sysstat* table, or the *v$resource_limit* view (only after release 8.1.7, because of a bug).

RAM used by Oracle Connections

We have seen that an isolated memory region called the Program Global Area (PGA) is allocated in UNIX RAM memory whenever a dedicated connection is made to Oracle. The PGA consists of the following areas:

- **Sort area** - This is the largest and most important area of the PGA.

- **Session information** – This small area allows the user connection to communicate with the Oracle database by storing the internal connection addresses.

- **Cursor state** – This area stores all re-entrant values for the executing connection.

- **Stack space** - This area contains miscellaneous control structures.

Oracle has the ability to dynamically change the largest component of a PGA, the sort area size, at either the system-level or the session-level. For example, here are some Oracle9i commands to dynamically change the sort area:

```
alter session set sort_area_size=10m deferred;
alter system  set sort_area_size=10m;
```

The *alter session* command instructs UNIX to expand the PGA sort area as the sort requires. If external PGA RAM is used, Oracle issues the *malloc()* command, creating a RAM sort area. The RAM sort area is not allocated until the retrieval from the databases has been completed, and the memory only exists for the duration of the sort. In this way, the RAM is only allocated when Oracle needs it, and the memory demands on the server are reduced.

Determining the Optimal PGA Size

Our sample MS-Windows server has 1,250 megabytes of RAM. Subtracting 20 percent for overhead, we have 1000 megabytes available for Oracle.

Each PGA RAM region size is determined as follows:

- **OS Overhead** – We reserve 2 MB for Windows and 1 MB for UNIX.

- *Sort_area_size* **parameter value** – This RAM is used for data row sorting inside the PGA.

- *Hash_area_size* **parameter value** – This RAM defaults to 1.5 times *sort_area_size* and is used for performing hash joins of Oracle tables.

The values for *sort_area_size* and *hash_area_size* are quickly shown with the Oracle *show parameters* command:

```
SQL> show parameters area_size

NAME                                 TYPE         VALUE
------------------------------------ -----------  ---------
bitmap_merge_area_size               integer      1048576
create_bitmap_area_size              integer      8388608
hash_area_size                       integer      1048576
sort_area_size                       integer      524288
workarea_size_policy                 string       MANUAL
```

A quick dictionary query (*pga_size_each.sql*) against the *v$parameter* view will yield the correct value for each PGA RAM region size.

pga_size_each.sql

```
set pages 999;

column pga_size format 999,999,999

select
    2048576+a.value+b.value    pga_size
from
    v$parameter a,
    v$parameter b
where
    a.name = 'sort_area_size'
and
    b.name = 'hash_area_size'
;
```

The data dictionary query output shows that the Oracle PGA will use 3.6 megabytes of RAM memory for each connected Oracle session.

```
    PGA_SIZE
------------
   3,621,440
```

Creating a Self-Tuning Oracle Database

If we now multiply the number of connected users by the PGA demands for each user, we will know exactly how much RAM should be reserved for connected sessions. Alternatively, we could issue an SQL statement to obtain the same result. The script for such a statement is shown below.

A Script for Computing Total PGA RAM

This script reads both the *sort_area_size* and *hash_area_size* to compute the total PGA region. The script will display a prompt for the high water mark of connected users and then computes the total PGA RAM to reserve for dedicated Oracle connections. The MS-Windows PGA session incurs a 2 MB overhead in this example.

pga_size.sql

```
--  ****************************************************************
-- Compute PGA sizes
--
-- Copyright (c) 2003 By Donald K. Burleson - All Rights reserved.
--  ****************************************************************

set pages 999;

column pga_size format 999,999,999

accept hwm number prompt 'Enter the high-water mark of connected
users: '

select
    &hwm*(2048576+a.value+b.value) pga_size
from
    v$parameter a,
    v$parameter b
where
    a.name = 'sort_area_size'
and
    b.name = 'hash_area_size'
;
```

Running the script, we see that we are prompted for the high water mark. We will assume that the HWM of connected sessions to the Oracle database server is 100.

Oracle will do the math and display the amount of RAM to reserve for Oracle connections.

```
SQL> @pga_size

Enter the high-water mark of connected users: 100

old    2:      &hwm*(2048576+a.value+b.value) pga_size
new    2:            100*(2048576+a.value+b.value) pga_size


PGA_SIZE
------------
 362,144,000
```

Returning to our example Windows server, we are ready to calculate the optimum SGA size. Multiplying 100 by the amount needed for each PGA region (3.62 MB) and adding the 2 MB PGA overhead, gives us the total PGA size of 364 MB. The maximum size for the SGA is determined by subtracting the total PGA and the OS overhead from the total RAM on the server. Here is a summary:

```
Total RAM on Windows Server           1250 MB

Less:

Total PGA regions for 100 users:       364 MB
RAM reserved for Windows (20%)         250 MB
                                      ----------
Maximum SGA Size                       636 MB
```

This leaves 636 MB of free memory for the SGA. Therefore, the RAM allocated to the data buffers should be adjusted to make the SGA size less than 636 MB. If the SGA size is greater than 636 MB, the server will begin to page RAM, impairing the performance of the entire server. We also see that the total Oracle RAM is 1000 MB, equivalent to the total PGA plus the total SGA.

Always remember, RAM is an expensive database server resource, and the DBA has the responsibility to fully allocate RAM resources on the server. RAM that is not utilized wastes expensive hardware resources, and RAM depreciates regardless of usage.

Conclusion

To summarize, the size of an Oracle SGA is primarily based on the following parameter settings:

- *shared_pool_size* – Sets the amount of Oracle administrative RAM and the library cache.

- *db_cache_size* – Sets the amount of RAM memory for the data buffers.

- *large_pool_size* – Sets the size of the Java pool.

- *log_buffer* – Sets the size of the redo log RAM buffers.

Generally, *db_cache_size* is the most variable of these parameters. Most DBAs place additional RAM in the *db_cache_size* because of the nearly insatiable appetite that Oracle has for data buffers.

This chapter has discussed the major issues involving Oracle RAM configuration, and the salient points include:

- Un-used RAM on a dedicated Oracle server is an expensive wasted resource.

- The Oracle DBA must manage the expensive RAM resources and insure that the various Oracle components are configured with the proper amount of RAM.

- The DBA can accurately estimate the total amount of usable RAM on a dedicated Oracle server.

- The total Oracle RAM for all dedicated database connections is the SGA size plus the PGA RAM.

- It is easy to see the amount of RAM on the Oracle server with a few simple OS commands.

Now that we understand the basic principles involved in sizing RAM regions for the Oracle SGA, let's take a closer look at the methods and commands for modifying those regions.

Chapter 2

Oracle9i Self-tuning Basics

Starting with Oracle9i, almost all Oracle parameters can be dynamically changed using *alter system* commands. This provides the Oracle DBA with the ability to grow and shrink areas of the Oracle RAM region, based upon the existing processing demands. More importantly, this ability lays the foundation for the creation of a self-tuning Oracle9i database.

To illustrate, consider the following example with a 16K data buffer experiencing a poor data buffer hit ratio, while the 32K buffer has a good data buffer hit ratio (Figure 2.1)

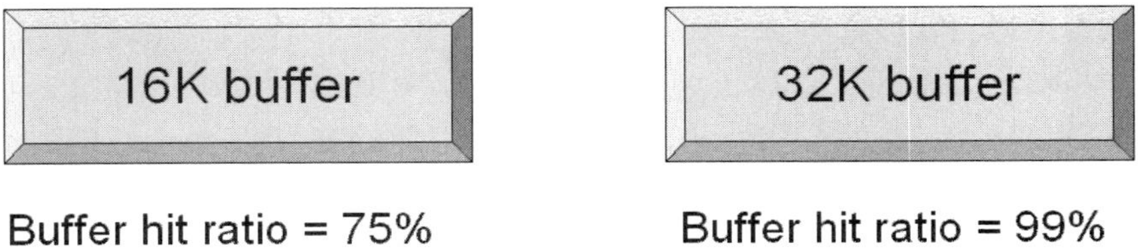

16K buffer	32K buffer
Buffer hit ratio = 75%	Buffer hit ratio = 99%

Figure 2.1 – Over-allocated and under-allocated RAM regions

Using *alter system* commands, we can adjust the RAM frames between the data buffers to reduce disk I/O and improve RAM efficiency for the 16K data buffer (Figure 2.2)

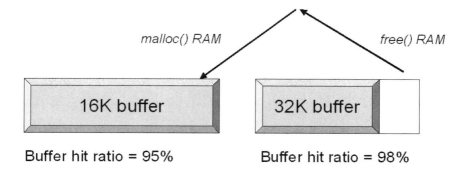

Buffer hit ratio = 95%   Buffer hit ratio = 98%

Figure 2.2 – Dynamic RAM adjustment in Oracle9i

Here is a script that adjusts the RAM caches. This script prompts the DBA for the name of the cache and the sizes and issues the appropriate *alter system* commands to adjust the regions.

```
SQL> @dyn_sga

Enter cache to decrease: shared_pool_size
Enter cache to increase: db_cache_size
Enter amount to change: 1048576

alter system set shared_pool_size = 49283072;
System altered.

alter system set db_cache_size = 17825792;
System altered.
```

Here is the source code for this handy script.

---

dyn_sga.sql

```
-- ********************************************************************
-- Dynamic SGA modification
--
-- Copyright (c) 2003 By Donald K. Burleson - All Rights reserved.
-- ********************************************************************
set heading off
set feedback off
set verify off

accept decrease_pool char    prompt 'Enter cache to decrease: '
accept increase_pool char    prompt 'Enter cache to increase: '
```

Creating a Self-Tuning Oracle Database

```
accept change_amount number prompt 'Enter amount to  change: `

spool run_sga.sql
select
   'alter system set &decrease_pool = '||to_char(to_number(value)-
&change_amount)||';'
from
   v$parameter
where
   name = lower('&decrease_pool');
select
   'alter system set &increase_pool =
'||to_char(to_number(value)+&change_amount)||';'
from
   v$parameter
where
   name = lower('&increase_pool';
spool off
set feedback on
@run_sga
```

While this technique is great for altering the sizes of the SGA regions, we can also use techniques to move database objects between tablespaces with different blocksizes.

For example, when Oracle9i detects an object with significant sequential block access and index access of a single block, that table or index can be scheduled for a move to a larger tablespace. All indexes perform best when defined with the largest supported block size for the environment (usually 32k blocks).

```
alter index
   cust_idx
rebuild
   tablespace 32k_tablespace;
```

In the case of indexes, a simple index move can cause a 16X reduction in physical disk I/O. (Figure 2.3)

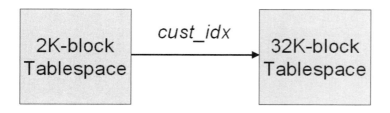

Figure 2.3 – The disk I/O reduction from tablespace relocation

Remember, Oracle indexes are almost always accessed via range scans, and large blocks minimize disk I/O. We can also use STATSPACK to monitor disk I/O and plot trends of read I/O and write I/O.

Once these I/O signatures are known, we can verify whether or not the increased I/O is legitimate. If the high disk I/O is legitimate (it is not the result of sub-optimal SQL), then we can schedule a re-allocation of SGA resources in anticipation of the trend. (Figure 2.4)

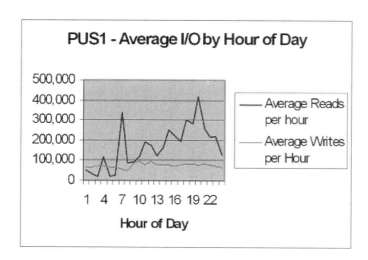

Figure 2.4 – A time-series average of disk I/O

Creating a Self-Tuning Oracle Database

Next, let's examine the most important area of monitoring, the RAM data buffers.

Monitoring the Data Buffers

Before you can self-tune the data buffers, you need a mechanism to monitor the data buffer hit ratio for all pools you have defined. You can monitor all 7 data buffers with this script:

---

bhr_all.sql

```
-- ****************************************************************
-- Display avg. BHR since database startup time
--
-- Copyright (c) 2003 By Donald K. Burleson - All Rights reserved.
-- ****************************************************************

select
   name,
   block_size,
   (1-(physical_reads/ decode(db_block_gets+consistent_gets, 0,
.001, db_block_gets+consistent_gets)))*100    cache_hit_ratio
from
   v$buffer_pool_statistics;
```

Here, we see the output from this script. Note that the names of the sized block buffers remain DEFAULT, and you must select the *block_size* column to differentiate between the buffers. Here we see al 7 data buffers.

NAME	BLOCK_SIZE	CACHE_HIT_RATIO
DEFAULT	32,767	.97
RECYCLE	16,384	.61
KEEP	16,384	1.00
DEFAULT	16,384	.92
DEFAULT	4,096	.99
DEFAULT	8,192	.98
DEFAULT	2,048	.86

Of course, this report is not very useful because the *v$sysstat* view only shows averages since the instance was started. To perform self-tuning of the data buffers, we can use Oracle's

---

STATSPACK utility to measure the data buffer hit ratios every hour.

To do this, we can use a STATSPACK data buffer exception report and the *stats$buffer_pool_statistics* table. The script that generated this listing is *rpt_bhr_all.sql*, and is presented in detail in Chapter 3. Figure 2.5 shows the output from a time-based data buffer hit ratio report.

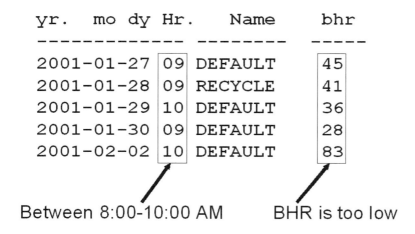

Figure 2.5 – Time-based proactive problem detection

In Figure 2.5 we see the database regularly experiences a decline in the data buffer hit ratio between 9:00-11:00 AM. Once we have confirmed that this is a "signature" and repeats on a regular basis, we can take action to correct this deficiency:

1. Review and tune all SQL between 9:00-11:00 AM, using the SQL source captured in the *stats$sql_summary* table.
2. Schedule a job (cron or *dbms_job*) to increase the *db_cache_size* during this period.

Next, let's look at how we can use scripts to detect changes in RAM sort and hash joins and take proactive self-tuning measures.

Oracle9i Sorting

As we have noted, a serious problem in Oracle8i was the requirement that all dedicated connections use a one-size-fits-all *sort_area_size*. Oracle9i now has the option of running automatic PGA memory management, and Oracle has introduced a new Oracle parameter called *pga_aggregate_target*.

When the *pga_aggregate_target* parameter is set and you are using dedicated Oracle connections, Oracle9i will ignore all of the PGA parameters in the Oracle file, including *sort_area_size*, *hash_area_size*, and *sort_area_retained_size*. On a dedicated Oracle server, Oracle recommends that the value of *pga_aggregate_target* be set to the amount of remaining memory (less a 10 percent overhead for other UNIX tasks) on the UNIX server after the instance has been started.

Once the *pga_aggregate_target* has been set, Oracle will automatically manage PGA memory allocation based upon the individual needs of each Oracle connection. Oracle9i allows the *pga_aggregate_target* parameter to be modified at the instance level with the *alter system* command, thereby allowing the DBA to dynamically adjust the total RAM region available to Oracle9i.

Oracle9i also introduces a new parameter called *workarea_size_policy*. When this parameter is set to *automatic*, all Oracle connections will benefit from the shared PGA memory. When *workarea_size_policy* is set to *manual*, connections will allocate memory according to the values for the *sort_area_size* parameter. Under the *automatic* mode, Oracle tries to maximize the number of work areas that are using optimal memory and uses one-pass memory for the others.

Oracle9i Views for PGA Management

Oracle9i has introduced several new views and new columns in existing views to aid in assessing the internal allocation of RAM memory in Oracle9i. The following new *v$* views can be used to monitor RAM memory usage of dedicated Oracle9i connections:

- **v$process** - Three new columns are added in Oracle9i for monitoring PGA memory usage. The new columns are called *pga_used_mem*, *pga_alloc_mem*, and *pga_max_mem*.

- **v$sysstat** - There are many new statistics rows, including work area statistics for optimal, one-pass, and multi-pass.

- **v$pgastat** - This new view shows internals of PGA memory usage for all background processes and dedicated connections.

- **v$sql_plan** - This exciting new view contains execution plan information for all currently executing SQL. This is a tremendous tool for the performance-tuning professional who must locate suboptimal SQL statements.

- ***v$workarea*** - This new view provides detailed cumulative statistics on RAM memory usage for Oracle9i connections.

- ***v$workarea_active*** - This new view shows internal RAM memory usage information for all currently executing SQL statements.

Let's take a closer look at these new Oracle9i features and scripts, which allow you to see detailed RAM memory usage.

The *v$sysstat* View

The following query gives the total number of work area executions and the percentage of time they were executed since the database instance was started, in these three modes:

---

work_area.sql

```
-- ***************************************************************
-- Display workarea executions
--
-- Copyright (c) 2003 By Donald K. Burleson - All Rights reserved.
-- ***************************************************************

select
    name                                          profile,
    cnt,
    decode(total, 0, 0, round(cnt*100/total)) percentage
from
    (
      select
         name,
         value cnt,
         (sum(value) over ()) total
      from
         v$sysstat
      where
         name like 'workarea exec%'
    );
```

The output of this query might look like the following:

```
PROFILE                              CNT         PERCENTAGE
----------------------------------   ----------  ----------
workarea executions - optimal             5395          95
workarea executions - onepass              284           5
workarea executions - multipass              0           0
```

The output of this query is used to tell the DBA when to dynamically adjust *pga_aggregate_target*. In general, the value of *pga_aggregate_target* should be increased when multi-pass executions are greater than zero, and reduced whenever the optimal executions are 100 percent.

The *v$pgastat* View

The *v$pgastat* view provides instance-level summary statistics on the PGA usage and the automatic memory manager. The following script provides excellent overall usage statistics for all Oracle9i connections:

---

check_pga.sql

```
-- ***************************************************************
-- Display detailed PGA statistics
--
-- Copyright (c) 2003 By Donald K. Burleson - All Rights reserved.
-- ***************************************************************
column name   format a30
column value format 999,999,999

select
   name,
   value
from
   v$pgastat
;
```

Creating a Self-Tuning Oracle Database

The output of this query might look like the following:

```
NAME                                        VALUE
------------------------------------------- ----------
aggregate PGA auto target                   736,052,224
global memory bound                              21,200
total expected memory                           141,144
total PGA inuse                              22,234,736
total PGA allocated                          55,327,872
maximum PGA allocated                        23,970,624
total PGA used for auto workareas               262,144
maximum PGA used for auto workareas           7,333,032
total PGA used for manual workareas                   0
maximum PGA used for manual workareas                 0
estimated PGA memory for optimal                141,395
maximum PGA memory for optimal              500,123,520
estimated PGA memory for one-pass               534,144
maximum PGA memory for one-pass              52,123,520
```

In the preceding display from *v$pgastat*, we see the following statistics:

- **Aggregate PGA auto target** - This column gives the total amount of available memory for Oracle9i connections. As we have already noted, this value is derived from the value on the Oracle parameter *pga_aggregate_target*.

- **Global memory bound** - This statistic measures the maximum size of a work area, and Oracle recommends that whenever this statistic drops below 1 megabyte, you should increase the value of the *pga_aggregate_target* parameter.

- **Total PGA allocated** - This statistic displays the high-water mark of all PGA memory usage on the database. You should see this value approach the value of *pga_aggregate_target* as usage increases.

- **Total PGA used for auto workareas** - This statistic monitors RAM consumption of all connections running in automatic memory mode. Remember, Oracle does not allow all internal processes to use the automatic memory feature. For example, Java and PL/SQL will allocate RAM memory, and it will not be counted in the total PGA statistic. Hence, you can subtract this value from the total PGA allocated to see the amount of memory used by connections and the RAM memory consumed by Java and PL/SQL.

- **Estimated PGA memory for optimal/one-pass** - This statistic estimates how much memory is required to execute all task connections demanded by RAM in optimal mode. Remember, when Oracle9i experiences a memory shortage, the DBA will invoke the multi-pass operation to attempt to locate recently-freed RAM memory. This statistic is critical for monitoring RAM consumption in Oracle9i, and most Oracle DBAs will increase *pga_aggregate_target* to this value.

The *v$process* View

The *v$process* view has been enhanced with several new columns to show automatic PGA usage, including *pga_used_mem*, *pga_alloc_mem*, and *pga_max_mem*. Here is a query to display these values:

```
select
   program,
   pga_used_mem,
   pga_alloc_mem,
   pga_max_mem
from
   v$process;
```

Creating a Self-Tuning Oracle Database

The output of this query might look like the following:

```
PROGRAM                        PGA_USED_MEM PGA_ALLOC_MEM PGA_MAX_MEM
----------------------------   ------------ ------------- -----------

oracle@janet (PMON)                 120463        234291      234291
oracle@janet (DBW0)                1307179       1817295     1817295
oracle@janet (LGWR)                4343655       4849203     4849203
oracle@janet (CKPT)                 194999        332583      332583
oracle@janet (SMON)                 179923        775311      775323
oracle@janet (RECO)                 129719        242803      242803
oracle@janet (TNS V1-V3)           1400543       1540627     1540915
oracle@janet (P000)                 299599        373791      635959
oracle@janet (P001)                 299599        373791      636007
oracle@janet (TNS V1-V3)           1400543       1540627     1540915
oracle@janet (TNS V1-V3)             22341       1716253     3625241
```

Here you see allocated, used, and maximum memory for all connections to Oracle. You can see the RAM demands of each of the background processes, and you also have detailed information about individual connections.

Note that it is possible to join the *v$process* view with the *v$sql_plan* table to look closer at the RAM memory demands of specific connections.

The v$workarea View

Oracle also has two new views to show active work area space, the *v$sql_workarea* and the *v$sql_workarea_active* views. The *v$sql_workarea_active* view will display all of the work areas that are currently executing in the instance. Note that small sorts (under 65,535 bytes) are excluded from the view. The *v$sql_workarea_active* view can be used to quickly monitor the size of all large active work areas.

```
-- ****************************************************************
-- Display PGA workarea details
--
-- Copyright (c) 2003 By Donald K. Burleson - All Rights reserved.
-- ****************************************************************

select
    to_number(decode(SID, 65535, NULL, SID))  sid,
    operation_type              OPERATION,
    trunc(WORK_AREA_SIZE/1024)  WSIZE,
    trunc(EXPECTED_SIZE/1024)   ESIZE,
    trunc(ACTUAL_MEM_USED/1024) MEM,
    trunc(MAX_MEM_USED/1024)    "MAX MEM",
    number_passes               PASS
from
    v$sql_workarea_active
order by
    1,2;
```

Here is a sample listing from this script:

```
SID OPERATION           WSIZE     ESIZE       MEM   MAX MEM PASS
--- ------------------- ----- --------- --------- --------- ----
 27 GROUP BY (SORT)        73        73        64        64    0
 44 HASH-JOIN            3148      3147      2437      6342    1
 71 HASH-JOIN           13241     19200     12884     34684    1
```

This output shows that session 44 is running a hash join whose work area is running in one-pass mode. This work area is currently using 2 megabytes of PGA memory and in the past, has used up to 6.5 megabytes.

This view is very useful for assessing the current memory operations within Oracle. You can use the SID column to join into the *v$process* and *v$session* views for additional information about each task.

Conclusion

This chapter has introduced mechanisms for self-tuning the Oracle9i database using proactive monitoring and automated SGA adjustment scripts. The main points of this chapter include:

- Simple SQL*Plus scripts can be used to allow the DBA to grow and shrink the SGA regions. These scripts can be automated and placed in cron or *dbms_job* for scheduled processing.

- The STATSPACK utility is a great way to monitor repeating deficiencies in the RAM regions.

- Oracle provides enhanced views in *v$process, v$workarea,* and *v$pgastat* to allow you to monitor the behavior of the RAM sort area within the *pga_aggregate_target.*

- The *v$* views in Oracle9i also provide insights about the RAM usage for individual SQL statements within the library cache.

Remember, even though the data buffers are important, they are not the sole indicator of good performance. For example, SQL tuning and event wait analysis are often far better for performance than tuning the Oracle data buffers.

Now we are ready to look deeper into self-tuning techniques. The next chapter will explore the mechanisms for monitoring and self-tuning the most important SGA areas of all, the data buffers.

Chapter 3

Oracle9i Data Buffer Internals

The increasing sophistication and flexibility of Oracle9i offers new challenges to the database administrator in trying to determine the optimal size of each SGA region. Making the proper decisions to efficiently utilize RAM resources can mean saving millions of dollars.

The single most important region for Oracle tuning is the data buffer cache, and the data buffers can easily be automated. To briefly review, the Oracle data buffers use RAM to cache incoming data blocks. The data can then be retrieved from RAM thousands of times faster than a disk access. Managing these RAM buffers intelligently will have a huge impact on Oracle performance.

Tuning the Oracle9i Data Buffer Pools

There were many new features in the Oracle9i database that were announced with fanfare in the publicity surrounding its introduction, but the ability to support multiple block sizes received comparatively little attention. As a result, the important role multiple block sizes play in reducing disk I/O was less appreciated than it might have been. For the Oracle administrator, multiple block sizes are extremely significant and exciting. For the first time, data buffer sizes can be customized to fit the specific needs of the database.

Prior to Oracle9i, the entire Oracle database had a single block size, and this size was determined at the time the database was created. Oracle8i did allow tables and index blocks to be segregated into three separate data buffers, but the buffer caches had to be the same size. The KEEP pool stored table blocks that were referenced frequently, the RECYCLE pool held blocks from large-table full-table scans, and the DEFAULT pool contained miscellaneous object blocks.

Oracle9i opens up a whole new world of disk I/O management with its ability to configure multiple block sizes. We can define tablespaces with block sizes of 2K, 4K, 8K, 16K, and 32K, and match these tablespaces with similar sized tables and indexes, minimizing disk I/O and efficiently managing wasted space in the data buffers. We now have a total of seven separate and distinct data buffers to segregate incoming table and index rows.

Many Oracle professionals still fail to appreciate the benefits of multiple block sizes and do not understand that the marginal cost of I/O for large blocks is negligible. A 32K block fetch costs only 1 percent more than a 2K block fetch because 99 percent of the disk I/O is involved with the read-write head and rotational delay in getting to the cylinder and track.

This is an important concept for Oracle indexes because indexes perform better when stored in large block size tablespaces. They perform better because the b-trees are better balanced, and there is less overall disk overhead with sequential index node access. Let's begin our exploration of this important new feature with a review of data caching in Oracle9i.

Data Block Caching in the SGA

When an SQL statement makes a row request, Oracle first checks the internal memory to see if the data is already in a data buffer, thereby avoiding unnecessary disk I/O. Now that very large SGAs are available with 64-bit versions of Oracle, small databases can be entirely cached, and one data buffer can be defined for each database block. For databases that are too large to be stored in data buffers, Oracle has developed a scheme to retain the most frequently used RAM blocks.

When the data buffer does not have enough room for the whole database, Oracle utilizes a least-recently-used algorithm that selects pages to flush from memory. Oracle assigns each block in the data buffer an in-memory control structure. The incoming data block is placed in the middle of the data buffer. Every time the block is requested, it moves to the front of the list. Data blocks referenced infrequently will eventually reach the end of the data buffer, where they will be erased, thereby making room for new data blocks, as shown in Figure 3.1.

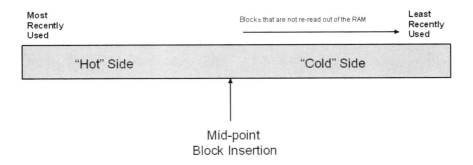

Figure 3.1 - Aging data blocks from the RAM block buffer

Beginning with Oracle8, Oracle provided three separate pools of RAM (the KEEP, RECYCLE, and DEFAULT pools) in the *db_cache_size* region to hold incoming data blocks. With Oracle8i, Oracle dramatically changed the way data blocks were handled within the buffers, inserting them into the midpoint of the block and dividing the block into "hot" and "cold" areas. Oracle 7 had always placed incoming blocks at the most recently used end of the buffer. With Oracle9i, the highly efficient technique of prioritizing data blocks within the buffers is combined with the additional flexibility of multiple block sizes.

To view the current database buffer parameters, we can use SQL*Plus to issue the *show parameters buffer* command. A list of parameters from an Oracle8i database is shown below.

```
SVRMGR> show parameters buffer

NAME                                 TYPE      VALUE
------------------------------------ --------- ---------------------
buffer_pool_keep                     string    500
buffer_pool_recycle                  string
db_block_buffers                     integer   6000
log_archive_buffer_size              integer   64
log_archive_buffers                  integer   4
log_buffer                           integer   2048000
sort_write_buffer_size               integer   32768
sort_write_buffers                   integer   2
use_indirect_data_buffers            boolean   FALSE
```

Here we see the KEEP pool (*buffer_pool_keep*), the RECYCLE pool (*buffer_pool_recycle*) and the DEFAULT pool (*db_cache_size*).

The same listing for an Oracle9i database is shown here:

```
SQL> show parameters buffer

NAME                                TYPE     VALUE
----------------------------------- -------- ------
buffer_pool_keep                    string
buffer_pool_recycle                 string
db_block_buffers                    integer  0
log_buffer                          integer  524288
use_indirect_data_buffers           boolean  FALSE
```

Full Table Caching in Oracle9i

The large RAM region within Oracle8i made it possible to fully cache an entire database. Before Oracle introduced their 64-bit versions, the maximum size of the SGA was 1.7 gigabytes on many UNIX platforms. With the advent of 64-bit addressing, there is no practical limitation on the size of an Oracle SGA, and there are enough data buffers for the DBA to cache the whole database.

The benefits of full data caching become clear when we recall that retrieving data from RAM is an order of magnitude faster than reading it from disk. It was mentioned earlier that access time from disks is expressed in milliseconds, while RAM speed is expressed in nanoseconds. In Oracle9i, RAM cache access is at least 2,000 times faster than disk access.

If the DBA intends to fully cache an Oracle database, he must plan carefully. The multiple data buffer pools are not needed, and most DBAs cache all the data blocks in the DEFAULT pool.

In general, any database less than 20 gigabytes is fully cached today, while larger databases still require partial data buffer caches. The DBA can issue the following simple command to calculate the number of allocated data blocks:

```
SQL> select
  2      sum(blocks)
  3  from
  4      dba_data_files;

SUM(BLOCKS)
-----------
     217360

SQL> select
  2      sum(blocks)
  3  from
  4*     dba_extents

SUM(BLOCKS)
-----------
     127723
```

The actual number of blocks being used can only be determined by looking at DBMS_ROWID for actual block addresses.

```
select
   sum(blocks)
from
   dba_data_files;
```

The DBA must carefully monitor the database as it expands in order to increase the *db_cache_size*, but this approach insures that all read activity is fully cached. When the database is started, the DBA will invoke a script to load the buffers for all of the database tables, usually by issuing a *select count(*) from xxx* command.

This technique insures that all data blocks are cached for reads, but write activity still requires disk I/O. With RAM becoming cheaper each year, the trend of fully caching smaller databases will continue.

The Data Buffer Hit Ratio (DBHR)

The goal of the administrator is to keep as many of the frequently used Oracle blocks in buffer memory as possible. The data buffer hit ratio (DBHR) measures how often requested data blocks are found in the buffer pool. In sum, the DBHR is the ratio of logical reads to physical disk reads. As the hit ratio approaches 100 percent, more data blocks are found in memory, resulting in fewer disk I/Os and faster overall database performance.

On the other hand, if the data buffer hit ratio falls below 90 percent, fewer data blocks are resident in memory, requiring Oracle to perform a disk I/O to move them into the data buffer. The formula for calculating the DBHR in Oracle8 was:

```
1 - (Physical Reads - Physical Reads Direct)
    -----------------------------------------
       (session logical reads)
```

It should be noted that the formula for calculating the hit ratio in Oracle7 and Oracle8 does not include direct block reads. Direct block reads become a separate statistic in Oracle8i.

It is important to realize that the data buffer hit ratio is only one small part of Oracle tuning. You should also use STATSPACK, interrogate system wait events, and tune your SQL for optimal execution plans.

The hit ratio for Oracle8i can be gathered from the *v$* views, as shown below. However, the value is not very useful because it shows the total buffer hit ratio since the beginning of the instance.

```
select
   1 - ((a.value - (b.value))/d.value) "Cache Hit Ratio"
from
   v$sysstat a,
   v$sysstat b,
   v$sysstat d
where
   a.name='physical reads'
and
   b.name='physical reads direct'
and
   d.name='session logical reads';
```

Many novice DBAs make the mistake of using the DBHR from the *v$* views. The *v$buffer_pool_statistics* view does contain the accumulated values for data buffer pool usage, but computing the data buffer hit ratio from the *v$* tables only provides the average since the database was started.

In order for the DBA to determine how well the buffer pools are performing, it is necessary to measure the hit ratio at more frequent intervals. Calculating the DBHR for Oracle8 and beyond is more complicated than earlier versions, but the results enable the administrator to achieve a higher level of tuning than was previously possible.

In the next section, we will look at the wealth of information that STATSPACK can provide for tracking buffer pool utilization and computing the data buffer hit ratio.

Using STATSPACK for the Data Buffer Hit Ratio

STATSPACK uses the *stats$buffer_pool_statistics* table for monitoring buffer pool statistics. This table contains the following useful columns:

- **name** - This column shows the name of the data buffer (KEEP, RECYCLE, or DEFAULT).

- **free_buffer_wait** - This is a count of the number of waits on free buffers.

- **buffer_busy_wait** - This is the number of times a requested block was in the data buffer but unavailable because of a conflict.

- **db_block_gets** - This is the number of database block gets, which are either logical or physical.

- **consistent_gets** - This is the number of logical reads.

- **physical_reads** - This is the number of disk block fetch requests issued by Oracle. (Remember, this is not always a "real" read because of disk array caching.)

- **physical_writes** - This is the number of physical disk write requests from Oracle. If you have a disk array, the actual writes are performed asynchronously.

These STATSPACK columns provide information that can be used to measure several important metrics, including the most important, the data buffer hit ratio.

Data Buffer Monitoring with STATSPACK

There are two ways to use STATSPACK to compute the data buffer hit ratio. In Oracle8i and beyond, we may use the *stats$buffer_pool_statistics* table. For Oracle 8.0, the *stats$sesstat* table should be used.

NOTE: There is an important difference between *stats$buffer_pool_statistics* in Oracle 8.0 and Oracle8i. If STATSPACK was back-ported into Oracle 8.0, the *stats$buffer_pool_statistics* view does not give accurate data buffer hit ratios for the DEFAULT, KEEP, and RECYCLE pools. Instead, there is only one pool defined as FAKE VIEW. This uses the *stats$sysstat* table and should be used for Oracle 8.0:

---

rpt_bhr.sql

```
-- ****************************************************************
-- Display BHR for Oracle8
--
-- Copyright (c) 2003 By Donald K. Burleson - All Rights reserved.
-- ****************************************************************

set pages 9999;

column logical_reads   format 999,999,999
column phys_reads      format 999,999,999
column phys_writes     format 999,999,999
column "BUFFER HIT RATIO" format 999

select
   to_char(snap_time,'yyyy-mm-dd HH24'),
   a.value + b.value  "logical_reads",
   c.value            "phys_reads",
   d.value            "phys_writes",
   round(100 * (((a.value-e.value)+(b.value-f.value))-(c.value-
g.value)) /
(a.value-e.value)+(b.value-f.v
value)))
         "BUFFER HIT RATIO"
from
   perfstat.stats$sysstat a,
   perfstat.stats$sysstat b,
   perfstat.stats$sysstat c,
   perfstat.stats$sysstat d,
   perfstat.stats$sysstat e,
   perfstat.stats$sysstat f,
   perfstat.stats$sysstat g,
   perfstat.stats$snapshot    sn
where
   a.snap_id = sn.snap_id
and
   b.snap_id = sn.snap_id
and
   c.snap_id = sn.snap_id
and
   d.snap_id = sn.snap_id
```

```
and
   e.snap_id = sn.snap_id-1
and
   f.snap_id = sn.snap_id-1
and
   g.snap_id = sn.snap_id-1
and
   a.statistic# = 39
and
   e.statistic# = 39
and
   b.statistic# = 38
and
   f.statistic# = 38
and
   c.statistic# = 40
and
   g.statistic# = 40
and
   d.statistic# = 41
;
```

The method below is used for Oracle 8.1 and beyond:

rpt_bhr_all.sql

```
-- ********************************************************************
-- Display BHR for Oracle8i & beyond
--
-- Copyright (c) 2003 By Donald K. Burleson - All Rights reserved.
-- ********************************************************************

column bhr format 9.99
column mydate heading 'yr.  mo dy Hr.'

select
   to_char(snap_time,'yyyy-mm-dd HH24')      mydate,
   new.name                                  buffer_pool_name,
   (((new.consistent_gets-old.consistent_gets)+
   (new.db_block_gets-old.db_block_gets))-
   (new.physical_reads-old.physical_reads))
   /
   ((new.consistent_gets-old.consistent_gets)+
   (new.db_block_gets-old.db_block_gets))    bhr
from
   perfstat.stats$buffer_pool_statistics old,
   perfstat.stats$buffer_pool_statistics new,
   perfstat.stats$snapshot               sn
where
   (((new.consistent_gets-old.consistent_gets)+
   (new.db_block_gets-old.db_block_gets))-
   (new.physical_reads-old.physical_reads))
   /
   ((new.consistent_gets-old.consistent_gets)+
   (new.db_block_gets-old.db_block_gets)) < .90
and
```

```
   new.name = old.name
and
   new.snap_id = sn.snap_id
and
   old.snap_id = sn.snap_id-1
;
```

A sample output from this script is shown below:

```
yr.  mo dy Hr BUFFER_POOL_NAME        BHR
------------- -------------------- -----
2001-12-12 15 DEFAULT                .92
2001-12-12 15 KEEP                   .99
2001-12-12 15 RECYCLE                .75
2001-12-12 16 DEFAULT                .94
2001-12-12 16 KEEP                   .99
2001-12-12 16 RECYCLE                .65
```

This script provides us with the data buffer hit ratio for each of the buffer pools at one-hour intervals. It is important that the KEEP pool always has a 99-100 percent DBHR. If this is not the case, data blocks should be added to the KEEP pool to make it the same size as the sum of all object data blocks that are assigned to the KEEP pool.

To summarize, the DBA can control the data buffer hit ratio by adding blocks within the Oracle parameters. Oracle recommends that the DBHR not fall below 90 percent.

The DBA will notice that in practice, variation in the data buffer hit ratio will increase with the frequency of measured intervals. For example, STATSPACK may report a DBHR of 92 percent at hourly intervals, but indicate wide variation when the ratio is sampled in two-minute intervals, as shown in Figure 3.2.

For details on performing tuning with STATSPACK, see the book *Oracle9i High-Performance Tuning with STATSPACK* by Oracle Press.

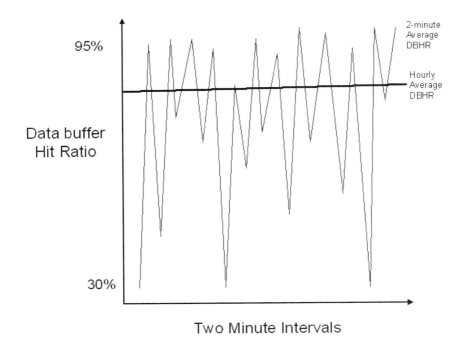

Figure 3.2 - Sampling the data buffer hit ratio over two-minute intervals

We can understand how this variation occurs by considering a simple example. Suppose a database instance is started, and the first ten tasks read ten separate blocks. At this point, the data buffer hit ratio is zero because all the requested blocks had to be retrieved via a physical disk I/O. In general, data warehouses will have lower buffer hit ratios because they are exposed to large-table full-table scans, while OLTP databases will have higher buffer hit ratios because the indexes used most frequently are cached in the data buffer.

A good guiding principle for the Oracle DBA is that as much RAM as possible should be allocated to the data buffers without causing the server to page-in RAM. Blocks should be added to the data buffers whenever the hourly hit ratio falls below 90 percent.

Oracle's Seven Data Buffer Hit Ratios

We have seen that the data buffer hit ratio is a common metric used by Oracle tuning experts to measure the propensity of a row to be in the data buffer. For example, a hit ratio of 95 percent means that 95 percent of row requests were already present in the data buffer, thereby avoiding an expensive disk I/O. In general, as the size of the data buffers is increased, the DBHR will also increase and approach 100 percent.

Oracle9i has a separate data buffer hit ratio for all seven data buffer caches. For optimum performance, the Oracle DBA should constantly monitor all seven data buffers and adjust their size, based on each data buffer hit ratio. Oracle9i provides the exciting feature of allowing the number of RAM buffers within any of the data buffer caches to be changed dynamically.

This is done through *alter system* commands that allow the size of the buffers to be changed while Oracle remains available. This means that the DBA can maximize performance in response to current statistics by manually de-allocating RAM from one data buffer and shifting it to another buffer cache.

The general rule is that the more data that can be retrieved from a single I/O, the better the overall hit ratio. However, we need to delve a little deeper to get a more complete understanding of how multiple data buffers operate.

Allocating Oracle9i Data Buffer Caches

Let's take a look at how multiple data buffers actually work. As an example, we might define the following buffer cache allocations in our initialization parameters.

```
db_block_size=32768          -- This is the system-wide
                             -- default block size

db_cache_size=3G             -- This allocates a total of 3
                             -- gigabytes for all of the 32K
                             -- data buffers

db_keep_cache_size=1G        -- Use 1 gigabyte for the KEEP pool

db_recycle_cache_size=500M   -- Here is 500 meg for the RECYCLE pool
                             -- Hence, the DEFAULT pool is 1,500 meg


-- ***************************************************************
-- The caches below are all additional RAM memory (total=3.1 gig)
-- that are above and beyond the allocation from db_cache_size
-- ***************************************************************

db_2k_cache_size=200M        -- This cache is reserved for random
                             -- block retrieval on tables that
                             -- have small rows.

db_4k_cache_size=500M        -- This 4K buffer will be reserved
                             -- exclusively for tables with a small
                             -- average row length and random access

db_8k_cache_size=800M        -- This is a separate cache for
                             -- segregating I/O for specific tables

db_16k_cache_size=1600M      -- This is a separate cache for
                             -- segregating I/O for specific tables
```

What is the total RAM allocated to the data buffer caches in the example above? The total RAM is the sum of all named buffer caches, plus *db_cache_size*. Hence, the total RAM in the example is 6,100 megabytes, or 6.1 gigabytes.

Remember, as subsets of the DEFAULT pool, the *db_keep_cache_size* and *db_recycle_cache_size* are subtracted from the *db_cache_size*. After subtracting the allocation for the KEEP and RECYCLE pools, the DEFAULT pool is

1.5 gigabytes in our example. Of course, the total size must be less than the value of *sga_max_size*.

Also, bear in mind that the assigned value of *db_block_size* is the default block size and cannot be used for another buffer. The *db_block_size* is 32K in our example, so we cannot allocate a *db_32k_cache_size*.

We have now defined seven totally separate data buffers. Table 3.1 lists each buffer, its total size, its defined block size, and the number of data blocks each buffer can hold.

NAME	SIZE	BLOCK SIZE	BLOCK SPACE
KEEP pool	1,000 MB	32K	31,250 blocks
RECYCLE pool	500 MB	32K	15,625 blocks
DEFAULT pool	1,500 MB	32K	46,875 blocks
2k cache	200 MB	2K	100,000 blocks
4k cache	500 MB	4K	125,000 blocks
8k cache	800 MB	8K	100,000 blocks
16k cache	1,600 MB	16K	100,000 blocks

Table 3.1 - Computing the block space for multiple data buffer caches

The next step is to create tablespaces for each of the block sizes. Oracle will then automatically load the tablespace blocks into the data buffer of the appropriate block size.

To illustrate, we mentioned that the *db_2k_cache_size* is suitable for tables comprised of small row sizes that are always accessed randomly. Small block sizes are also effective in preventing DML locking problems with bitmap indexes. Hence, we could define a 2K tablespace as follows:

```
create tablespace
   2k_tablespace
datafile
   '/u01/oradata/mysid/2k_file.dbf'
size
   100M
blocksize
   2k
;
```

Once the *db_2k_cache_size* data buffer is defined, Oracle will always load the *2k_tablespace* blocks into it. We can use the *Create Table As Select* (CTAS) command to move all the appropriate tables into the new tablespace as shown:

```
-- ******************************************
-- First, disable all RI constraints
-- ******************************************
alter table customer disable constraint fk_cust_name;

-- ******************************************
-- Copy the table into a new tablespace
-- ******************************************
create table
   new_customer
as select
   *
from
   customer
tablespace
   2k_tablespace
;

-- ******************************************
-- Rename the tables
-- ******************************************
rename customer to old_customer;
rename new_customer to customer;

-- ******************************************
-- Lastly, you must now transfer all RI constraints and indexes
-- ******************************************
create index pk_cust_idx on customer . . . ;
alter table customer add constraint fk_cust . . . ;
```

Now that we understand the basic concepts behind the data buffers, let's go deeper into the internals and see how STATSPACK data can allow us to monitor and self-tune the data buffers.

Creating a Self-Tuning Oracle Database

Data Buffer Monitoring

Determining the optimal size for the data buffers is a critical task for large databases. It is economically prohibitive to cache an entire database in RAM as databases grow ever larger, perhaps reaching sizes in the hundreds of billions of bytes. The difficulty Oracle professionals face is finding the point of diminishing marginal returns as they allocate additional RAM resources to the database. Successfully determining that point and effectively optimizing RAM can save a company hundreds of thousands, if not millions, of dollars in RAM expenses.

Among the new features that Oracle9i provides to aid the administrator in this task is the *v$db_cache_advice* view. This view can help predict the benefit of adding buffers to the data buffer cache. It estimates the miss rate for twenty potential buffer cache sizes, throughout a range of 10 percent of the current size to 200 percent of the current size. This tool allows the Oracle DBA to accurately predict the optimal size for each RAM data buffer. A few examples will help illustrate the process.

In order to use the new view, RAM memory must be pre-allocated to the data buffers, just as it was in the Oracle7 *x$kcbcbh* utility. Setting the *init.ora* parameter *db_cache_advice* to the value of "on" or "ready" enables the cache advice feature. The DBA can set these values while the database is running with the alter system command, taking advantage of the predictive feature dynamically.

However, since the additional RAM buffers must be pre-allocated before the *db_cache_size* can use *v$db_cache_advice*, the DBA may wish to use the utility only once to determine the optimal size.

How Does it Work?

Figure 3.3 graphically shows that a marginal increase in data buffer blocks is asymptotic to disk I/O. A large reduction in disk I/O is achieved with a small increase in the size of a small RAM buffer.

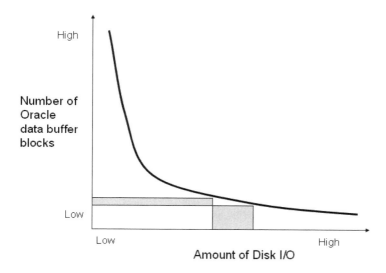

Figure 3.3 – The reduction in disk I/O from an increase to RAM data buffer.

Here, we see that a small increase in the size of *db_cache_size* results in a large reduction in actual disk I/O. This happens because the cache is small and frequently referenced data blocks are now able to stay resident in the RAM data buffer.

However, we can see that the impressive reduction in disk I/O does not continue indefinitely. As the total RAM size begins to approach the database size, the marginal reduction in disk I/O begins to decline (Figure 3.4).

This low marginal cost is because all databases have data that is accessed infrequently. Infrequently accessed data does not normally have a bearing on the repeated reads performed by traditional OLTP applications, and this is why we see a marked decline in the marginal benefit as we approach full RAM caching of the database.

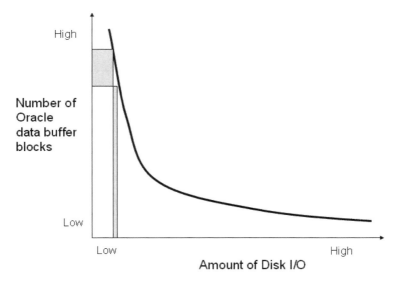

Figure 3.4 – Large buffers changes result in small I/O gains

As a general guideline, all memory available on the host should be tuned, and the *db_cache_size* should be allocating RAM resources up to the point of diminishing returns (Figure 3.5). This is the point where additional buffer blocks do not significantly improve the buffer hit ratio.

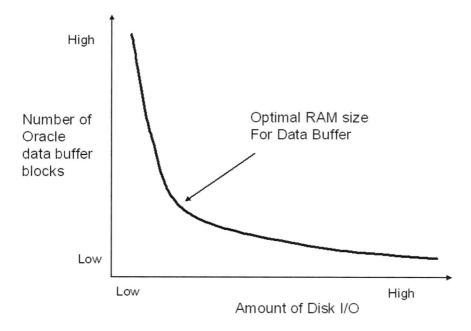

Figure 3.5- The optimal size of the RAM data buffer

The new *v$db_cache_advice* view is similar to an Oracle7 utility that also predicted the benefit of adding data buffers. The Oracle7 utility used the *x$kcbrbh* view to track buffer hits and the *x$kcbcbh* view to track buffer misses.

Bear in mind that the data buffer hit ratio can provide data similar to *v$db_cache_advice*, and most Oracle tuning professionals use both tools to monitor the effectiveness of their data buffers.

The following query can be used to perform the cache advice function, once the *db_cache_advice* has been enabled and the database has run long enough to give representative results.

Creating a Self-Tuning Oracle Database

```
cache_advice.sql
```

```
-- ******************************************************************
-- Display cache advice
--
-- Copyright (c) 2003 By Donald K. Burleson - All Rights reserved.
-- ******************************************************************



column c1    heading 'Cache Size (m)'         format 999,999,999,999
column c2    heading 'Buffers'                 format 999,999,999
column c3    heading 'Estd Phys|Read Factor'   format 999.90
column c4    heading 'Estd Phys| Reads'        format 999,999,999

select
   size_for_estimate           c1,
   buffers_for_estimate        c2,
   estd_physical_read_factor   c3,
   estd_physical_reads         c4
from
   v$db_cache_advice
where
   name = 'DEFAULT'
and
   block_size   = (SELECT value FROM V$PARAMETER
                   WHERE name = 'db_block_size')
and
   advice_status = 'ON';
```

The output from the script is shown below. Note that the values range from 10 percent of the current size to double the current size of the *db_cache_size* (Figure 3.1).

Cache Size (MB)	Buffers	Estd Phys Read Factor	Estd Phys Reads	
30	3,802	18.70	192,317,943	← 10% size
60	7,604	12.83	131,949,536	
91	11,406	7.38	75,865,861	
121	15,208	4.97	51,111,658	
152	19,010	3.64	37,460,786	
182	22,812	2.50	25,668,196	
212	26,614	1.74	17,850,847	
243	30,416	1.33	13,720,149	
273	34,218	1.13	11,583,180	
304	38,020	1.00	10,282,475	Current Size
334	41,822	.93	9,515,878	
364	45,624	.87	8,909,026	
395	49,426	.83	8,495,039	
424	53,228	.79	8,116,496	
456	57,030	.76	7,824,764	
486	60,832	.74	7,563,180	
517	64,634	.71	7,311,729	

```
547        68,436        .69    7,104,280
577        72,238        .67    6,895,122
608        76,040        .66    6,739,731  ← 2x size
```

Listing 3.1 – Output from db_cache_advice

The output shows neither a peak in total disk I/O nor a marginal trend with additional buffer RAM. This result is typical of a data warehouse database that reads large tables with full-table scans. In this case, there is no specific "optimal" setting for the *db_cache_size* parameter. Oracle will devour as much data buffer RAM as we feed to it, and disk I/O will continue to decline. However, there is no tangential line that indicates a point of diminishing returns for this application.

Taking the above into account, the thrifty DBA will apply this simple rule: *db_cache_size* should be increased if spare memory is available and marginal gains can be achieved by adding buffers. Of course, increasing the buffer blocks increases the amount of RAM running on the database. Hence, the database management system may place more demands on the processor than it can handle. The administrator must carefully juggle the amount of available memory with the limitations of the hardware in determining the optimal size of buffer blocks.

The DBA should prepare a strategy for enabling cache advice. If he sets *dba_cache_advice=on* while the database is running, Oracle will grab RAM pages from the shared pool RAM area, with potentially disastrous consequences for the objects in the library cache. If the existing *db_cache_size* setting is 500 megabytes, Oracle will grab a significant amount of RAM from the shared pool. For this reason, the DBA should set *db_cache_advice=ready* in the *init.ora* file, and the RAM memory will be pre-allocated by Oracle when the database is started.

For complex databases that can benefit from Oracle's sophistication, the DBA controls not only the gross size of the buffers, but also the block size of each individual buffer. For example, suppose the database tends to cluster records on a single database block, while the other data blocks remain small. Realizing that the I/O for a 32K block is virtually the same as the I/O for a 4K block, the database designer might choose to make some of the buffers larger to minimize I/O contention.

With the cache advice utility, Oracle9i provides the DBA with another tool to streamline database performance by predicting the optimal size of the RAM buffer pools.

Now that we understand the basics of buffer block size allocation, let's take a closer look at the internal mechanisms of the data buffers.

Internals of the Oracle Data Buffers

This section is a little more advanced and explores the internal mechanisms of the Oracle data buffers.

Oracle has long provided RAM buffers to prevent expensive data block re-reads from disk. But the way the buffers internally handle the incoming data has evolved radically. Prior to Oracle8i, an incoming data block was placed at the front of the list in the buffer. Oracle8i and beyond place the incoming block in the middle of the buffer chain.

Oracle keeps track of the touch count of the block after it is loaded. If a block receives multiple touches, it is moved closer to the head of the current list, guaranteeing that it is resident in RAM for a longer time period. New blocks are inserted into the middle of the buffer and their positions are adjusted according to access activity. This scheme effectively partitions each data buffer into two sections, a "hot" section that contains the data used most recently, and a "cold" section containing the data used least recently.

This is a tremendous advance over the earlier buffers. The midpoint insertion method essentially creates two sub-regions within the KEEP, RECYCLE, and DEFAULT pools. Each buffer pool has a hot and cold area, and only the data blocks that are requested repeatedly will migrate into the hot area of each pool. This method greatly improves the efficiency of the data buffers.

The size of the hot regions is internally configured by three hidden parameters:

_db_percent_hot_default
_db_percent_hot_keep
_db_percent_hot_recycle

Oracle Corporation does not recommend changing these parameters. They should only be altered by advanced DBAs who thoroughly understand the internal mechanisms of data buffers and wish to alter the performance of the buffers.

Finding Hot Blocks inside the Oracle Data Buffers

The relative performance of the data buffer pools is shown in Oracle8i by the internal *x$bh view*. This view shows the following columns:

- **tim** – The *tim* column governs the amount of time between touches and is related to the new *db_aging_touch_time* parameter.

- **tch** – The *tch* column gives the number of times a buffer is touched by user accesses. This is the count that directly relates to the promotion of buffers from the cold region into the hot, based on having been touched the number of times specified by the *db_againg_hot_criteria* parameter.

Since the *tch* column gives the number of touches for a specific data block, the hot blocks within the buffer can be displayed with a simple dictionary query:

high_buf_touch.sql

```
SELECT
   obj        object,
   dbarfil    file#,
   dbablk     block#,
   tch        touches
FROM
   x$bh
WHERE
   tch > 10
ORDER BY
   tch desc;
```

This advanced query is especially useful for tracking objects in the DEFAULT pool. It was pointed out earlier that there should be enough data blocks in the KEEP pool to fully cache the table or index. If we find hot blocks in the DEFAULT pool, they should be moved into the KEEP pool.

We are now ready to learn a technique for viewing the actual objects inside the data buffers and the scripts that will show their contents.

Viewing the Data Buffer Contents

The Oracle *v$bh* view shows the contents of the data buffers, as well as the number of blocks for each type of segment in the buffer. This view is primarily useful for indicating the amount of table and index caching in multiple data blocks. Combining the *v$bh* view with *dba_objects* and *dba_segments* provides a block-by-block listing of the data buffer contents and indicates how well the buffers are caching tables and indexes. Of course, this is very important in Oracle9i, since the data buffer sizes can be altered dynamically.

There are several data dictionary tricks when writing a script for mapping data objects to RAM buffers:

- **Duplicate object names** - When joining *dba_objects* to *dba_segments*, the name, type, and owner are all required to distinguish the object sufficiently.

- **Multiple blocksizes** – To show objects in the separate instantiated buffers (*db_2k_cache_size*, etc.), we need to display the block size for the object. We do this by computing the block size from *dba_segments*, dividing bytes by blocks.

- **Partitions** - With a standard equi-join, every object partition joins to every segment partition for a particular object. Hence, the following qualification is required to handle partitions:

```
and nvl(t1.subobject_name,'*') = nvl(s.partition_name,'*')
```

- **Clusters** – Clusters present a challenge when joining the *v$bh* row with its corresponding database object. Instead of joining the *bh.objd* to *object_id*, we need to join into *data_object_id*.

- **Multiple caches** - There are situations where a particular block may be cached more than once in the buffer cache. This is a mystifying concept, but it is easily overcome by creating the following in-line view:

```
(select distinct objd, file#, block# from v$bh where status
!= 'free')
```

This is the most important script in this text because it provides a detailed analysis of those objects in the data buffers. This information is critical when considering an alteration to the data buffer sizes.

Many thanks to Randy Cunningham for the developing this sophisticated and powerful script. Please note that the script below only works with Oracle9i.

---

buf_blocks.sql

```
set pages 999
set lines 92

ttitle 'Contents of Data Buffers'

drop table t1;

create table t1 as
select
    o.owner        owner,
```

```
     o.object_name        object_name,
     o.subobject_name subobject_name,
     o.object_type        object_type,
     count(distinct file# || block#)          num_blocks
from
     dba_objects  o,
     v$bh         bh
where
     o.data_object_id  = bh.objd
and
     o.owner not in ('SYS','SYSTEM')
and
     bh.status != 'free'
group by
     o.owner,
     o.object_name,
     o.subobject_name,
     o.object_type
order by
     count(distinct file# || block#) desc
;

column c0 heading "Owner"                                  format a12
column c1 heading "Object|Name"                            format a30
column c2 heading "Object|Type"                            format a8
column c3 heading "Number of|Blocks in|Buffer|Cache"       format 99,999,999
column c4 heading "Percentage|of object|blocks in|Buffer"  format 999
column c5 heading "Buffer|Pool"                            format a7
column c6 heading "Block|Size"                             format 99,999

select
     t1.owner                                       c0,
     object_name                                    c1,
     case when object_type = 'TABLE PARTITION' then 'TAB PART'
          when object_type = 'INDEX PARTITION' then 'IDX PART'
          else object_type end c2,
     sum(num_blocks)                                c3,
     (sum(num_blocks)/greatest(sum(blocks), .001))*100 c4,
     buffer_pool                                    c5,
     sum(bytes)/sum(blocks)                         c6
from
     t1,
     dba_segments s
where
     s.segment_name = t1.object_name
and
     s.owner = t1.owner
and
     s.segment_type = t1.object_type
and
     nvl(s.partition_name,'-') = nvl(t1.subobject_name,'-')
group by
     t1.owner,
     object_name,
     object_type,
     buffer_pool
having
     sum(num_blocks) > 10
order by
     sum(num_blocks) desc
;
```

A sample listing from this exciting report is shown below. We can see that the report lists the tables and indexes that reside inside the data buffer. This is important information for the Oracle professional who needs to know how many blocks for each object reside in the RAM buffer. To effectively manage the limited RAM resources, the Oracle

DBA must be able to know the ramifications of decreasing the size of the data buffer caches.

Here is the report from *buf_blocks.sql* when run against a large Oracle data warehouse (Listing 3.2).

```
                          Contents of Data Buffers

                                      Number of Percentage
                                      Blocks in of object
                     Object          Object    Buffer     Buffer   Buffer    Block
    Owner            Name            Type       Cache     Blocks   Pool      Size
    ------------     --------------  ---------  -------   --------  -------   -------
    DW01             WORKORDER       TAB PART   94,856         6   DEFAULT    8,192
    DW01             HOUSE           TAB PART   50,674         7   DEFAULT   16,384
    ODSA             WORKORDER       TABLE      28,481         2   DEFAULT   16,384
    DW01             SUBSCRIBER      TAB PART   23,237         3   DEFAULT    4,096
    ODS              WORKORDER       TABLE      19,926         1   DEFAULT    8,192
    DW01             WRKR_ACCT_IDX   INDEX       8,525         5   DEFAULT   16,384
    DW01             SUSC_SVCC_IDX   INDEX       8,453        38   KEEP      32,768
    DW02             WRKR_DTEN_IDX   IDX PART    6,035         6   KEEP      32,768
    DW02             SUSC_SVCC_IDX   INDEX       5,485        25   DEFAULT   16,384
    DW02             WRKR_LCDT_IDX   IDX PART    5,149         5   DEFAULT   16,384
    DW01             WORKORDER_CODE  TABLE       5,000         0   RECYCLE   32,768
    DW01             WRKR_LCDT_IDX   IDX PART    4,929         4   KEEP      32,768
    DW02             WOSC_SCDE_IDX   INDEX       4,479         6   KEEP      32,768
    DW01             SBSC_ACCT_IDX   INDEX       4,439         8   DEFAULT   32,768
    DW02             WRKR_WKTP_IDX   IDX PART    3,825         7   KEEP      32,768
    DB_AUDIT         CUSTOMER_AUDIT  TABLE       3,301        99   DEFAULT    4,096
    DW01             WRKR_CLSS_IDX   IDX PART    2,984         5   KEEP      32,768
    DW01             WRKR_AHWO_IDX   INDEX       2,838         2   DEFAULT   32,768
    DW01             WRKR_DTEN_IDX   IDX PART    2,801         5   KEEP      32,768
```

Listing 3.2 – Specific objects in the Oracle RAM data buffers

This is an interesting report because we see three object types (tables, indexes, and partitions), and we also see the sub-sets of the DEFAULT pool for KEEP and RECYCLE. Also, note that all indexes are defined in the largest supported block size (*db_32k_cache_size*), and multiple buffer pools of 4K, 8K, 16K and 32K sizes are defined.

The output of this script is somewhat confusing because of the repeated DEFAULT buffer pool name. This is misleading because the KEEP and RECYCLE buffer pools are sub-sets of *db_cache_size* and can ONLY accommodate objects with the DEFAULT *db_block_size*.

Conversely, any block sizes that are NOT the default *db_block_size*, go into the buffer pool named DEFAULT. As you can see from the output listing, there are really 6 mutually exclusive and independently-sized buffer pools, and four of them are called "DEFAULT."

It is interesting to run this report repeatedly because the Oracle data buffers are so dynamic. Running the script frequently allows us to view the blocks entering and leaving the data buffer. We can see the midpoint insertion method in action and the hot and cold regions as they update. Each time a block is re-referenced it moves to the head of the MRU chain on the hot side of the data buffer. Blocks that are accessed less frequently will age-out, first moving into the cold region and eventually being paged-out to make room for new incoming blocks.

This *buf_blocks.sql* script is even more important when considering a decrease to a cache size. When you issue an *alter system* command to decrease the cache size, Oracle will grab pages from the least recently used (LRU) end of the buffer. Depending on the amount of RAM removed, an *alter system* command will un-cache data blocks that may be needed by upcoming SQL statements.

In the next section, we will look more closely at the KEEP and RECYCLE data buffers and how objects are selected for inclusion.

Inside the KEEP and RECYCLE Pools

We have already seen that Oracle8 began providing three separate pools of RAM in the *db_cache_size* area to hold incoming data blocks. Let's look at them in a little more depth:

- **KEEP pool** – The KEEP pool holds tables that are referenced frequently by the application. This typically includes small tables that have frequent full-table scans and reference tables, and objects that are normally more than 80% cached in the data buffers. The KEEP pool is the evolved form of the table cache command in Oracle7.

- **RECYCLE pool** – The RECYCLE pool is reserved for large-table full-table scans. Data blocks from full-table scans are unlikely to be re-read. Segregating these blocks into their own special pool prevents more frequently used tables and indexes from being flushed out of the system.

- **DEFAULT pool** – The DEFAULT pool stores all other tables and indexes that do not fit the KEEP or RECYCLE criteria.

Bear in mind that the KEEP and RECYCLE pools are subsets of the DEFAULT pool.

Locating Tables and Indexes for the KEEP Pool

According to Oracle documentation, *"A good candidate for a segment to put into the KEEP pool is a segment that is smaller than 10% of the size of the DEFAULT buffer pool and has incurred at least 1% of the total I/Os in the system"*. More concisely, a small table that is in high demand is a good candidate for KEEP caching.

How can we locate small tables that are subject to full-table scans? The best method is to search the SQL that is currently in the library cache. Oracle can then generate a report that lists all the full-table scans in the database at that time.

The script below examines the execution plans of *plan9i.sql* and reports on the frequency of full-table scans.

plan9i.sql

```
--***********************************************************
-- Object Access script report
--
-- © 2003 by Donald K. Burleson
--
--   No part of this SQL script may be copied. Sold or distributed
--   without the express consent of Donald K. Burleson
--***********************************************************


-- ***********************************************************
-- Report section
-- ***********************************************************

set echo off;
set feedback on

set pages 999;
column nbr_FTS    format 999,999
column num_rows format 999,999,999
column blocks    format 999,999
column owner     format a14;
column name      format a24;
column ch        format a1;

column object_owner heading "Owner"            format a12;
column ct           heading "# of SQL selects" format 999,999;

select
   object_owner,
   count(*)    ct
from
   v$sql_plan
where
   object_owner is not null
group by
   object_owner
order by
   ct desc
;
--spool access.lst;
```

```
set heading off;
set feedback off;

set heading on;
set feedback on;
ttitle 'full table scans and counts|  |The "K" indicates that the
table is in the KEEP Pool (Oracle8).'
select
   p.owner,
   p.name,
   t.num_rows,
--    ltrim(t.cache) ch,
   decode(t.buffer_pool,'KEEP','Y','DEFAULT','N') K,
   s.blocks blocks,
   sum(a.executions) nbr_FTS
from
   dba_tables    t,
   dba_segments s,
   v$sqlarea     a,
   (select distinct
     address,
     object_owner owner,
     object_name name
   from
     v$sql_plan
   where
     operation = 'TABLE ACCESS'
     and
     options = 'FULL') p
where
   a.address = p.address
   and
   t.owner = s.owner
   and
   t.table_name = s.segment_name
   and
   t.table_name = p.name
   and
   t.owner = p.owner
   and
   t.owner not in ('SYS','SYSTEM')
having
   sum(a.executions) > 9
group by
   p.owner, p.name, t.num_rows, t.cache, t.buffer_pool, s.blocks
order by
   sum(a.executions) desc;

column nbr_RID  format 999,999,999
column num_rows format 999,999,999
column owner    format a15;
column name     format a25;

ttitle 'Table access by ROWID and counts'
select
   p.owner,
   p.name,
   t.num_rows,
   sum(s.executions) nbr_RID
```

```
from
   dba_tables t,
   v$sqlarea s,
   (select distinct
      address,
      object_owner owner,
      object_name name
   from
      v$sql_plan
   where
      operation = 'TABLE ACCESS'
      and
      options = 'BY ROWID') p
where
   s.address = p.address
   and
   t.table_name = p.name
   and
   t.owner = p.owner
having
   sum(s.executions) > 9
group by
   p.owner, p.name, t.num_rows
order by
   sum(s.executions) desc;

--*****************************************************
--   Index Report Section
--*****************************************************

column nbr_scans  format 999,999,999
column num_rows   format 999,999,999
column tbl_blocks format 999,999,999
column owner      format a9;
column table_name format a20;
column index_name format a20;

ttitle 'Index full scans and counts'
select
   p.owner,
   d.table_name,
   p.name index_name,
   seg.blocks tbl_blocks,
   sum(s.executions) nbr_scans
from
   dba_segments seg,
   v$sqlarea s,
   dba_indexes d,
   (select distinct
      address,
      object_owner owner,
      object_name name
   from
      v$sql_plan
   where
      operation = 'INDEX'
      and
      options = 'FULL SCAN') p
where
```

```
      d.index_name = p.name
      and
      s.address = p.address
      and
      d.table_name = seg.segment_name
      and
      seg.owner = p.owner
having
      sum(s.executions) > 9
group by
      p.owner, d.table_name, p.name, seg.blocks
order by
      sum(s.executions) desc;


ttitle 'Index range scans and counts'
select
      p.owner,
      d.table_name,
      p.name index_name,
      seg.blocks tbl_blocks,
      sum(s.executions) nbr_scans
from
      dba_segments seg,
      v$sqlarea s,
      dba_indexes d,
     (select distinct
        address,
        object_owner owner,
        object_name name
      from
        v$sql_plan

      where
        operation = 'INDEX'
        and
        options = 'RANGE SCAN') p
where
      d.index_name = p.name
      and
      s.address = p.address
      and
      d.table_name = seg.segment_name
      and
      seg.owner = p.owner
having
      sum(s.executions) > 9
group by
      p.owner, d.table_name, p.name, seg.blocks
order by
      sum(s.executions) desc;


ttitle 'Index unique scans and counts'
select
      p.owner,
      d.table_name,
      p.name index_name,
      sum(s.executions) nbr_scans
```

```
from
   v$sqlarea s,
   dba_indexes d,
  (select distinct
     address,
     object_owner owner,
     object_name name
   from
     v$sql_plan
   where
     operation = 'INDEX'
     and
     options = 'UNIQUE SCAN') p
where
   d.index_name = p.name
   and
   s.address = p.address
having
   sum(s.executions) > 9
group by
   p.owner, d.table_name, p.name
order by
   sum(s.executions) desc;
```

These reports use the following columns:

- **OWNER** - The schema owner for the table.

- **NAME** - The table name from *dba_tables*.

- **NUM_ROWS** - The number of rows in the table as of the last *compute statistics* from *dba_tables*.

- **C** (Oracle7 only) – An Oracle7 column that displays Y if the table is cached, N if it is not cached.

- **K** (Oracle8+ only) – Displays "K" if the table is assigned to the KEEP pool.

- **BLOCKS** – Number of blocks in the table as defined in *dba_segments* .

- **NBR_FTS** – The number of full-table scans against the table.

This report gives all the information needed to select candidate tables for the KEEP pool. The database will benefit from placing small tables (less than 2 percent of *db_cache_size*) that are subject to frequent full-table scans in the KEEP pool. The report from an Oracle Applications database below shows full-table scans on both large and small tables (Listing 3.3).

Full table scans and counts

OWNER	NAME	NUM_ROWS	C	K	BLOCKS	NBR_FTS
APPLSYS	FND_CONC_RELEASE_DISJS	39	N	K	2	98,864
APPLSYS	FND_CONC_RELEASE_PERIODS	39	N	K	2	98,864
APPLSYS	FND_CONC_RELEASE_STATES	1	N	K	2	98,864
APPLSYS	FND_CONC_PP_ACTIONS	7,021	N		1,262	52,036
APPLSYS	FND_CONC_REL_CONJ_MEMBER	0	N	K	22	50,174
APPLSYS	FND_CONC_REL_DISJ_MEMBER	39	N	K	2	50,174
APPLSYS	FND_FILE_TEMP	0	N		22	48,611
APPLSYS	FND_RUN_REQUESTS	99	N		32	48,606
INV	MTL_PARAMETERS	6	N	K	6	21,478
APPLSYS	FND_PRODUCT_GROUPS	1	N		2	12,555
APPLSYS	FND_CONCURRENT_QUEUES_TL	13	N	K	10	12,257
AP	AP_SYSTEM_PARAMETERS_ALL	1	N	K	6	4,521

Listing 3.3 – Full-table scans and counts for current SQL

Examining this report, we can quickly identify three files that should be moved to the KEEP pool by selecting the tables with less than 50 blocks that have no "K" designation.

Oracle developed the KEEP pool in order to fully cache blocks from frequently accessed tables and indexes in a separate buffer. When determining the size of the KEEP pool, the number of bytes comprising all tables that will reside in the KEEP area must be totaled. This will insure that the KEEP buffer is large enough to fully cache all the tables that have been assigned to it.

Oracle9i requires that a table only reside in a tablespace of the same block size as the buffer assigned to the table. For example, if the DEFAULT buffer is set at 32K, the alter command below would not work if the customer table resides in a 16K tablespace. Recall that the DEFAULT, KEEP, and RECYCLE designations only apply to the default block size; KEEP and RECYCLE buffers cannot be assigned different sizes than the default *db_block_size*.

```
alter table CUSTOMER storage (buffer_pool KEEP);
```

The whole point of the KEEP pool is to always have a data buffer hit ratio of 100 percent. The block size of the KEEP pool is not important because all blocks, once loaded, will remain in RAM memory. A KEEP pool might be defined as a 32K block size because a large RECYCLE buffer was needed to improve the performance of full-table scans.

CAUTION: Selecting tables for the KEEP pool is an iterative process. These reports include only SQL that happens to be in the library cache at the time of the report.

We emphasize that since our goal for the data buffer hit ratio of the KEEP pool is 100 percent, each time a table is added to KEEP, the number of blocks in that table must also be added to the KEEP pool parameter in the Oracle file.

Besides the full-table scan report, we can generate a report that shows every index access within SQL currently residing in the library cache.

The script output below shows how Oracle uses indexes to access Oracle tables (Listing 3.4).

Index range scans and counts

OWNER NBR_SCANS	TABLE_NAME	INDEX_NAME	TBL_BLOCKS	
SYS	JOB$	I_JOB_NEXT	3	4,755
SYS	OBJ$	I_OBJ2	778	945
SYS	ACCESS$	I_ACCESS1	478	787
SYS	DEPEN	I_DEPENDENCY1	878	787
SYS	IDL_SB4$	I_IDL_SB41	1,103	437
SYS	IDL_UB1$	I_IDL_UB11	26,653	411
SYS	IDL_CHAR$	I_IDL_CHAR1	653	410
SYS	IDL_UB2$	I_IDL_UB21	2,503	410
SYS	ARGUMENT$	I_ARGUMENT2	828	109
SYS	OBJAUTH$	I_OBJAUTH1	131	96

Index unique scans and counts

OWNER	TABLE_NAME	INDEX_NAME	NBR_SCANS
SYS	OBJ$	I_OBJ1	946
SYS	C_OBJ#	I_OBJ#	337
SYS	JAVASNM$	I_JAVASNM1	127
SYS	C_COBJ#	I_COBJ#	114
SYS	C_FILE#_BLOCK#	I_FILE#_BLOCK#	114
SYS	C_USER#	I_USER#	97
SYS	PROCEDUREJAVA$	I_PROCEDUREJAVA$	93
SYS	SMON_SCN_TO_TIME	SMON_SCN_TO_TIME_IDX	78
SYS	C_TS#	I_TS#	49
SYS	FILE$	I_FILE2	37
SYS	USER$	I_USER1	37
SYS	IND$	I_IND1	35
SYS	TRIGGER$	I_TRIGGER2	25
SYS	PROCEDURE$	I_PROCEDURE1	19
SYS	SYN$	I_SYN1	13
SYS	VIEW$	I_VIEW1	10

Listing 3.4 – Index access methods and counts for current SQL

Now that we can identify and locate small-table, full-table scans, let's see how we can quickly move small tables and indexes into the KEEP pool. We will use a data dictionary query to automatically generate KEEP and RECYCLE syntax.

Automatically Generate KEEP Syntax

Extrapolating from the above script, we can write another script that automatically identifies candidates for the KEEP pool and generates the syntax to move the tables into the pool.

The placement criteria for tables and indexes into the KEEP buffer are straightforward:

- **Small tables** – Parameters may be adjusted in the script based upon needs.

- **Experiences full-table scans** – Oracle designates the table as small and chooses a full-table scan over an index access.

- **Frequently-accessed tables** – The threshold for access can be adjusted in the script.

- **High buffer residency** – Any table that has more than 80% of its blocks in the data buffer should be cached in the KEEP pool.

There are two approaches to identifying tables for the KEEP pool:

- Tables (and associated indexes) that are small and have frequent full-table scans

- Objects that have more than 80% of their data blocks in the buffer

Here are scripts for each method.

Caching Small-table Full-table Scans in the KEEP Pool

Here is the first method that examines all execution plans, searching for small-table full-table scans. This is the script to automatically generate the KEEP syntax for any small table (you adjust the table size threshold) for tables that have many full-table scans.

9i_keep_syntax.sql

```
-- ****************************************************************
-- Create KEEP Pool syntax for small,
-- frequently-references tables & indexes
--
-- Copyright (c) 2003 By Donald K. Burleson - All Rights reserved.
-- ****************************************************************


-- ****************************************************************
-- Generate KEEP pool syntax for appropriate tables & indexes
-- ****************************************************************

set pages 999;
set heading off;
set feedback off;
ttitle off;

spool keep_syntax.sql

-- ****************************************************************
-- First, get the table list
-- ****************************************************************
select
   'alter table '||p.owner||'.'||p.name||' storage (buffer_pool
keep);'
from
   dba_tables    t,
   dba_segments  s,
   v$sqlarea     a,
   (select distinct
     address,
     object_owner owner,
     object_name name
   from
     v$sql_plan
   where
     operation = 'TABLE ACCESS'
     and
     options = 'FULL') p
where
   a.address = p.address
```

```
    and
    t.owner = s.owner
    and
    t.table_name = s.segment_name
    and
    t.table_name = p.name
    and
    t.owner = p.owner
    and
    t.owner not in ('SYS','SYSTEM')
    and
    t.buffer_pool <> 'KEEP'
having
    s.blocks < 50
group by
    p.owner, p.name, t.num_rows, s.blocks
UNION
-- ************************************************************
-- Next, get the index names
-- ************************************************************
select
    'alter index '||owner||'.'||index_name||' storage (buffer_pool
keep);'
from
    dba_indexes
where
    owner||'.'||table_name in
(
select
    p.owner||'.'||p.name
from
    dba_tables    t,
    dba_segments  s,
    v$sqlarea     a,
    (select distinct
      address,
      object_owner owner,
      object_name name
    from
      v$sql_plan
    where
      operation = 'TABLE ACCESS'
      and
      options = 'FULL') p
where
    a.address = p.address
    and
    t.owner = s.owner
    and
    t.table_name = s.segment_name
    and
    t.table_name = p.name
    and
    t.owner = p.owner
    and
    t.owner not in ('SYS','SYSTEM')
    and
    t.buffer_pool <> 'KEEP'
having
```

```
   s.blocks < 50
group by
   p.owner, p.name, t.num_rows, s.blocks
)
;


spool off;
```

Run the simple script below, and Oracle will generate the KEEP syntax.

```
alter index PUBS.BITMAP_BOOK_TYPE storage (buffer_pool keep);
alter index PUBS.BTREE_TITLE_TYPE storage (buffer_pool keep);
alter index PUBS.PK_BOOK storage (buffer_pool keep);
alter table PUBS.BOOK storage (buffer_pool keep);
alter table PUBS.BOOK_AUTHOR storage (buffer_pool keep);
alter table PUBS.PUBLISHER storage (buffer_pool keep);
alter table PUBS.SALES storage (buffer_pool keep);
```

Automating the Assignment of KEEP Pool Contents

Another method for identifying tables and indexes for the KEEP pool examines the current blocks in the data buffer. For this query, the rules are simple. Any object that has more than 80% of its data blocks in the data buffer should probably be fully cached.

It is highly unlikely that an undeserving table or index would meet this criterion. Of course, you would need to run this script at numerous times during the day because the buffer contents change very rapidly.

The following script can be run every hour via *dbms_job*, and automate the monitoring of KEEP pool candidates. Every time it finds a candidate, the DBA will execute the syntax and adjust the total KEEP pool size to accommodate the new object.

buf_keep_pool.sql

```
set pages 999

set lines 92


spool keep_syn.lst

drop table t1;

create table t1 as
select
    o.owner          owner,
    o.object_name    object_name,
    o.subobject_name subobject_name,
    o.object_type    object_type,
    count(distinct file# || block#)       num_blocks
from
    dba_objects  o,
    v$bh         bh
where
    o.data_object_id  = bh.objd
and
    o.owner not in ('SYS','SYSTEM')
and
    bh.status != 'free'
group by
    o.owner,
    o.object_name,
    o.subobject_name,
    o.object_type
order by
    count(distinct file# || block#) desc
;

select
    'alter '||s.segment_type||' '||t1.owner||'.'||s.segment_name||' storage (buffer_pool
keep);'
from
    t1,
    dba_segments s
where
    s.segment_name = t1.object_name
and
    s.owner = t1.owner
and
    s.segment_type = t1.object_type
and
    nvl(s.partition_name,'-') = nvl(t1.subobject_name,'-')
and
    buffer_pool <> 'KEEP'
and
    object_type in ('TABLE','INDEX')
group by
    s.segment_type,
    t1.owner,
    s.segment_name
having
    (sum(num_blocks)/greatest(sum(blocks), .001))*100 > 80
;


spool off;
```

Here is a sample of the output from this script.

```
alter TABLE BOM.BOM_DELETE_SUB_ENTITIES storage (buffer_pool keep);
alter TABLE BOM.BOM_OPERATIONAL_ROUTINGS storage (buffer_pool keep);
alter INDEX BOM.CST_ITEM_COSTS_U1 storage (buffer_pool keep);
alter TABLE APPLSYS.FND_CONCURRENT_PROGRAMS storage (buffer_pool keep);
alter TABLE APPLSYS.FND_CONCURRENT_REQUESTS storage (buffer_pool keep);
alter TABLE GL.GL_JE_BATCHES storage (buffer_pool keep);
alter INDEX GL.GL_JE_BATCHES_U2 storage (buffer_pool keep);
alter TABLE GL.GL_JE_HEADERS storage (buffer_pool keep);
alter TABLE INV.MTL_DEMAND_INTERFACE storage (buffer_pool keep);
alter INDEX INV.MTL_DEMAND_INTERFACE_N10 storage (buffer_pool keep);
alter TABLE INV.MTL_ITEM_CATEGORIES storage (buffer_pool keep);
alter TABLE INV.MTL_ONHAND_QUANTITIES storage (buffer_pool keep);
alter TABLE INV.MTL_SUPPLY_DEMAND_TEMP storage (buffer_pool keep);
alter TABLE PO.PO_REQUISITION_LINES_ALL storage (buffer_pool keep);
alter TABLE AR.RA_CUSTOMER_TRX_ALL storage (buffer_pool keep);
alter TABLE AR.RA_CUSTOMER_TRX_LINES_ALL storage (buffer_pool keep);
alter INDEX WIP.WIP_REQUIREMENT_OPERATIONS_N3 storage (buffer_pool keep);
```

In sum, there are two ways to identify tables and indexes for full caching in the KEEP pool. We start by explaining all of the SQL in the databases looking for small-table, full-table scans. Next, we repeatedly examine the data buffer cache, seeing any objects that have more than 80% of their blocks in RAM. Next, let's finish the job and see how to re-size the KEEP pool to accommodate your new objects.

Sizing the KEEP Pool

Finally, once the tables and indexes have been loaded into the KEEP buffer pool, the *buffer_pool_keep* parameter must be increased by the total number of blocks in the migrated tables.

The following script will total the number of blocks that the KEEP pool requires, insuring 100 percent data caching. You should note that the script adds 20 percent to the total to allow for growth in the cached objects. The DBA should run this important script frequently to make sure the KEEP pool always has a DBHR of 100 percent.

size_keep_pool.sql

```
-- **********************************************************
-- Display correct size for the KEEP pool
--
-- Copyright (c) 2003 By Donald K. Burleson - All Rights reserved.
-- **********************************************************

prompt The following will size your init.ora KEEP POOL,
prompt based on Oracle8 KEEP Pool assignment values
prompt

select
'BUFFER_POOL_KEEP = ('||trunc(sum(s.blocks)*1.2)||',2)'
from
   dba_segments s
where
   s.buffer_pool = 'KEEP';
;
```

This script outputs the Oracle parameter that resizes the KEEP pool for the next re-start of the Oracle instance. The parameter is placed in the *init.ora* file. You should know that Oracle9i deprecates *buffer_pool_keep* and it cannot be modified with an *alter system* command.

```
BUFFER_POOL_KEEP=(1456, 3)
```

We can now bounce the database and the parameter change will take effect.

STATSPACK Tables and KEEP Pool Data

The advanced Oracle professional can run sophisticated scripts to explain the SQL statements stored in the *stats$sql_summary* table. Using the default level-5 STATSPACK snapshots, the *stats$sql_summary* table will contain the top SQL statements that were in the library cache at the time of each hourly snapshot.

Alternatively, the *plan9i.sql* script can simply be modified to use the *stats$sql_summary* table instead of the *v$sqltext*.

Creating a Self-Tuning Oracle Database

Advanced KEEP Pool Candidate Identification

We have seen that the KEEP pool is an excellent storage location for small-table, full-table scans. It can also be a good place to store data blocks from frequently used segments that consume a lot of block space in the data buffers. These blocks are usually found within small reference tables that are accessed through an index and do not appear in the full-table scan report.

The *x$bh* internal view is the only window into the internals of the Oracle database buffers. The view contains much detailed information about the internal operations of the data buffer pools. Both the number of objects in a specific type and the number of touches for that object type can be counted in the *x$bh* table. It can even be used to create a snapshot of all the data blocks in the buffer.

The query shown below utilizes the *x$bh* view to identify all the objects that reside in blocks averaging over five touches and occupying over twenty blocks in the cache. It finds tables and indexes that are referenced frequently and are good candidates for inclusion in the KEEP pool.

hot_buffers.sql

```
--   ********************************************************************
-- Display hot buffer detail
--
-- Copyright (c) 2003 By Donald K. Burleson - All Rights reserved.
--   ********************************************************************
--
-- You MUST connect as SYS to run this script
connect sys/manager;

set lines 80;
set pages 999;

column avg_touches            format 999
column myname heading 'Name'  format a30
column mytype heading 'Type'  format a10
column buffers                format 999,999
```

```
SELECT
    object_type  mytype,
    object_name    myname,
    blocks,
    COUNT(1) buffers,
    AVG(tch) avg_touches
FROM
    sys.x$bh     a,
    dba_objects b,
    dba_segments s
WHERE
    a.obj = b.object_id
and
    b.object_name = s.segment_name
and
    b.owner not in ('SYS','SYSTEM')
GROUP BY
    object_name,
    object_type,
    blocks,
    obj
HAVING
    AVG(tch) > 5
AND
    COUNT(1) > 20;
```

The DBA should note that the *hot_buffers.sql* script would only run on Oracle8i and subsequent versions. This is because the *tch* column was not added until Oracle 8.1.6.

The output from the *hot_buffers.sql* script is shown next. It identifies the active objects within the data buffers based on the number of data blocks and the number of touches.

Type	Name	BLOCKS	BUFFERS	AVG_TOUCHES
TABLE	PAGE	104	107	44
TABLE	SUBSCRIPTION	192	22	52
INDEX	SEQ_KEY_IDX	40	34	47
TABLE	SEC_SESSIONS	80	172	70
TABLE	SEC_BROWSER_PROPERTIES	80	81	58
TABLE	EC_USER_SESSIONS	96	97	77
INDEX	SYS_C008245	32	29	270

Listing 3.5 – Hot buffer touches in the data buffers

The DBA must now decide whether the hot objects are to be segregated into the KEEP pool. In general, there

---

should be enough RAM available to store the entire table or index. Using the example, if we are considering adding the page table to the KEEP pool, we would need to add 104 blocks to the Oracle *buffer_pool_keep* parameter.

The results from this script will differ every time it is executed because the data buffers are dynamic, and data storage is transient. Some DBAs schedule this script as often as every minute, if they need to see exactly what is occurring inside the data buffers.

Automating KEEP Pool Assignment

As we noted earlier, the Oracle documentation states *"A good candidate for a segment to put into the KEEP pool is a segment that is smaller than 10% of the size of the DEFAULT buffer pool and has incurred at least 1% of the total I/Os in the system"*.

It is easy to locate segments that are less than 10% of the size of their data buffer, but Oracle does not have a mechanism to track I/O at the segment level. To get around this issue, some DBAs place each segment into an isolated tablespace, so that STATSPACK can show the total I/O. However, this is not a practical solution for complex schemas with hundreds of segments.

Since the idea of the KEEP is to fully cache the object, we want to locate those objects that are small and experience a disproportional amount of I/O activity. Using this guideline, there are two approaches, and unlike the recommendation from the Oracle documentation, these approaches can be completely automated:

- Cache tables & indexes where the table is small (<50 blocks) and the table experiences frequent full-table scans.

- Cache any objects that consume more than 10% of the size of their data buffer.

To identify these objects, we start by explaining all of the SQL in the databases looking for small-table, full-table scans. Next, we can repeatedly examine the data buffer cache, locating all objects that have more than 80% of their blocks in the data buffer cache.

The first method that uses *v$sql_plan* to examine all execution plans, searching for small-table, full-table scans, is found in *get_keep_pool.sql*. This can automatically generate the KEEP syntax for any small table (you adjust the table size threshold) for tables that have many full-table scans.

---

get_keep_pool.sql

```
-- ******************************************************************

-- Create KEEP Pool syntax for small,
-- frequently-references tables & indexes
--
-- Copyright (c) 2003 By Donald K. Burleson - All Rights reserved.
-- ******************************************************************

-- ************************************************************
-- Generate KEEP pool syntax for appropriate tables & indexes
-- ************************************************************

set pages 999;
set heading off;
set feedback off;
ttitle off;

spool keep_syntax.sql

-- ************************************************************
-- First, get the table list
-- ************************************************************
select
```

```
      'alter table '||p.owner||'.'||p.name||' storage (buffer_pool
keep);'
from
   dba_tables    t,
   dba_segments  s,
   v$sqlarea     a,
   (select distinct
     address,
     object_owner owner,
     object_name name
   from
     v$sql_plan
   where
     operation = 'TABLE ACCESS'
     and
     options = 'FULL') p
where
   a.address = p.address
   and
   t.owner = s.owner
   and
   t.table_name = s.segment_name
   and
   t.table_name = p.name
   and
   t.owner = p.owner
   and
   t.owner not in ('SYS','SYSTEM')
   and
   t.buffer_pool <> 'KEEP'
having
   s.blocks < 50
group by
   p.owner, p.name, t.num_rows, s.blocks
UNION
-- ************************************************************
-- Next, get the index names
-- ************************************************************
select
   'alter index '||owner||'.'||index_name||' storage (buffer_pool
keep);'
from
   dba_indexes
where
   owner||'.'||table_name in
(
select
   p.owner||'.'||p.name
from
   dba_tables    t,
   dba_segments  s,
   v$sqlarea     a,
   (select distinct
     address,
     object_owner owner,
     object_name name
   from
     v$sql_plan
   where
```

```
      operation = 'TABLE ACCESS'
      and
      options = 'FULL') p
where
   a.address = p.address
   and
   t.owner = s.owner
   and
   t.table_name = s.segment_name
   and
   t.table_name = p.name
   and
   t.owner = p.owner
   and
   t.owner not in ('SYS','SYSTEM')
   and
   t.buffer_pool <> 'KEEP'
having
   s.blocks < 50
group by
   p.owner, p.name, t.num_rows, s.blocks
)
;

spool off;
```

By running this script, we can use the Oracle9i *v$* views to generate our suggestions for the KEEP syntax, based on the number of blocks in the object.

```
alter index DING.PK_BOOK storage (buffer_pool keep);
alter table DING.BOOK storage (buffer_pool keep);
alter table DING.BOOK_AUTHOR storage (buffer_pool keep);
alter table DING.PUBLISHER storage (buffer_pool keep);
alter table DING.SALES storage (buffer_pool keep);
```

Another method for identifying tables and indexes for the KEEP pool examines the current blocks in the data buffer. For this query, the rules are simple. Any object that has more than 80% of its data blocks in the data buffer should probably be fully cached.

It is highly unlikely that an undeserving table or index would meet this criterion. Of course, you would need to run this script at numerous times during the day because the buffer contents change very rapidly.

The script in *keep_syn.sql* can be run every hour via *dbms_job*, and automate the monitoring of KEEP pool candidates. Every time it finds a candidate, the DBA will execute the syntax and adjust the total KEEP pool size to accommodate the new object. Here is the output from this script.

---

keep_syn.sql

```
set pages 999
set lines 92


spool keep_syn.lst

drop table t1;

create table t1 as
select
    o.owner          owner,
    o.object_name    object_name,
    o.subobject_name subobject_name,
    o.object_type    object_type,
    count(distinct file# || block#)          num_blocks
from
    dba_objects  o,
    v$bh         bh
where
    o.data_object_id  = bh.objd
and
    o.owner not in ('SYS','SYSTEM')
and
    bh.status != 'free'
group by
    o.owner,
    o.object_name,
    o.subobject_name,
    o.object_type
order by
    count(distinct file# || block#) desc
;

select
    'alter '||s.segment_type||' '||t1.owner||'.'||s.segment_name||'
storage (buffer_pool keep);'
from
    t1,
    dba_segments s
where
    s.segment_name = t1.object_name
and

    s.owner = t1.owner
and
```

```
   s.segment_type = t1.object_type
and
   nvl(s.partition_name,'-') = nvl(t1.subobject_name,'-')
and
   buffer_pool <> 'KEEP'
and
   object_type in ('TABLE','INDEX')
group by
   s.segment_type,
   t1.owner,
   s.segment_name
having
   (sum(num_blocks)/greatest(sum(blocks), .001))*100 > 80
;
```

Here is a sample of the output from this script:

```
alter TABLE IS.GL_JE_BATCHES storage (buffer_pool keep);
alter INDEX IS.GL_JE_BATCHES_U2 storage (buffer_pool keep);
alter TABLE IS.GL_JE_HEADERS storage (buffer_pool keep);
```

Once you have identified the segments for assignment to the KEEP pool, you will need to adjust the *db_keep_cache_size* parameter to ensure that it has enough blocks to fully cache all of the segments that are assigned to the pool.

Of course, there are many exceptions to this automated approach. For example, these scripts do not handle table partitions and other object types. Hence, these scripts should be used as a framework for your KEEP pool caching strategy, and should not be run as-is.

Now, let's look at scripts to automate the identification of objects for the RECYCLE pool. As we shall see in the next section, identifying candidates for the RECYCLE pool is very similar to the KEEP pool process.

Tuning the RECYCLE Pool

Oracle8 introduced the RECYCLE pool as a reusable data buffer for *transient data blocks*. Transient data blocks are blocks that are read as parts of large-table full-table scans and unlikely to soon be needed by Oracle again.

We want to use the RECYCLE pool for segregating large tables involved in frequent full-table scans. To locate these large-table full-table scans, we can return to the *plan9i.sql* full-table scan report:

```
                       full table scans and counts

OWNER        NAME                       NUM_ROWS C K    BLOCKS  NBR_FTS
----------   ------------------------   -------- - -   --------  -----
APPLSYS      FND_CONC_RELEASE_DISJS          39 N K          2   98,864
APPLSYS      FND_CONC_RELEASE_PERIODS        39 N K          2   98,864
APPLSYS      FND_CONC_RELEASE_STATES          1 N K          2   98,864
SYS          DUAL                               N K          2   63,466
APPLSYS      FND_CONC_PP_ACTIONS          7,021 N         1,262   52,036
APPLSYS      FND_CONC_REL_CONJ_MEMBER         0 N K         22   50,174
```

One table in the listing is a clear candidate for inclusion in the RECYCLE pool. The *fnd_conc_pp_actions* table contains 1,262 blocks and has experienced 52,036 full-table scans.

CAUTION: The prudent DBA should verify that the large-table full-table scan is legitimate before blindly assigning a table to the RECYCLE pool. Many queries are structured to perform full-table scans on tables, even though far less than 40 percent of the table rows will be referenced. A better-designed query will only perform large-table full-table scans in systems such as data warehouses that require frequent SUM or AVG queries that touch most or all of the table rows.

After candidates for the RECYCLE pool have been identified, we can run a script that reads the plan table generated from *plan9i.sql*. This query will search for large tables of over 10,000 blocks that are subject to full-table scans and are not already in the RECYCLE pool.

9i_recycle_syntax.sql

```
--  ****************************************************************
--  Generate RECYCLE pool syntax for appropriate tables & indexes
--
--  Copyright (c) 2003 By Donald K. Burleson - All Rights reserved.
--  ****************************************************************

set pages 999;
set heading off;
set feedback off;
ttitle off;

spool keep_syntax.sql

--  ************************************************************
--  First, get the table list
--  ************************************************************
select
   'alter table '||p.owner||'.'||p.name||' storage (buffer_pool
recycle);'
from
   dba_tables    t,
   dba_segments  s,
   v$sqlarea     a,
   (select distinct
     address,
     object_owner owner,
     object_name name
   from
      v$sql_plan
   where
      operation = 'TABLE ACCESS'
      and
      options = 'FULL') p
where
   a.address = p.address
   and
   t.owner = s.owner
   and
   t.table_name = s.segment_name
   and
   t.table_name = p.name
   and
   t.owner = p.owner
   and
   t.owner not in ('SYS','SYSTEM')
   and
   t.buffer_pool <> 'RECYCLE'
having
   s.blocks > 10000
group by
   p.owner, p.name, t.num_rows, s.blocks
UNION
--  ************************************************************
--  Next, get the index names
--  ************************************************************
```

```
select
   'alter index '||owner||'.'||index_name||' storage (buffer_pool
recycle);'
from
   dba_indexes
where
   owner||'.'||table_name in
(
select
   p.owner||'.'||p.name
from
   dba_tables    t,
   dba_segments s,
   v$sqlarea     a,
   (select distinct
     address,
     object_owner owner,
     object_name name
   from
     v$sql_plan
   where
     operation = 'TABLE ACCESS'
     and
     options = 'FULL') p
where
   a.address = p.address
   and
   t.owner = s.owner
   and
   t.table_name = s.segment_name
   and
   t.table_name = p.name
   and
   t.owner = p.owner
   and
   t.owner not in ('SYS','SYSTEM')
   and
   t.buffer_pool <> 'RECYCLE'
having
   s.blocks > 10000
group by
   p.owner, p.name, t.num_rows, s.blocks
)
;

spool off;
```

The output from this script is shown below:

```
SQL> @9i_recycle_syntax

alter table APPLSYS.FND_CONC_PP_ACTIONS storage (buffer_pool
recycle);
```

As a general rule, the DBA should check the SQL source to verify that a full-table query is retrieving over 40 percent of the table rows before adding any table to the RECYCLE pool.

We can use the *x$bh* view as another approach for finding RECYCLE candidates, just as we did for the KEEP pool. This topic is addressed in the next section.

Advanced RECYCLE Pool Tuning

The query below uses *x$bh.tch* to identify objects in the buffer cache that are larger than 5 percent of the total cache with single touch buffer counts. A significant amount of cache space is filled with these blocks that have only been used once. They are good candidates for inclusion in the RECYCLE buffer pool.

hot_recycle_blocks.sql

```
-- ********************************************************************
-- Display hot blocks in recycle pool
--
-- Copyright (c) 2003 By Donald K. Burleson - All Rights reserved.
-- ********************************************************************

set lines 80;
set pages 999;


column avg_touches format 999
column myname heading 'Name' format a30
column mytype heading 'Type' format a10
column buffers format 999,999

SELECT
    object_type    mytype,
    object_name      myname,
    blocks,
    COUNT(1) buffers,
    100*(COUNT(1)/totsize) pct_cache
FROM
    sys.x$bh      a,
    dba_objects b,
    dba_segments s,
    (select value totsize from v$parameter
         where name = 'db_cache_size')
WHERE
    a.obj = b.object_id
```

```
and
   tch=1   -- This line only works in 8.1.6 and above
and
   b.object_name = s.segment_name
and
   b.owner not in ('SYS','SYSTEM')
GROUP BY
   object_type,
   object_name,
   blocks,
   totsize
HAVING
   100*(COUNT(1)/totsize) > 5
;
```

We stress again that Oracle releases prior to 8.1.6 do not support the reference to the touch (*tch*) column. The report can still be useful with these releases, but there is no way of knowing how many times the objects have been touched since their entry into the data pool.

A sample report from this script is shown below. We see that these tables and indexes occupy over 5 percent of the data buffer space, and they have only been touched once. This behavior is characteristic of large-table, full-table scans.

Type	Name	BLOCKS	BUFFERS	PCT_CACHE
INDEX	WIP_REQUIREMENT_OPERATIONS_U1	1042	334	5.57
TABLE	MTL_DEMAND_INTERFACE	847	818	13.63
TABLE	MTL_SYSTEM_ITEMS	4227	493	8.22

To repeat, the DBA must take into consideration both the number of blocks in the table and how often the table appears in the query output, when determining whether to add objects to the RECYCLE pool.

Selecting candidates for the RECYCLE pool is an iterative process, just as it is for the KEEP pool. Data buffers are constantly changing, and the DBA may choose to run this script every minute over a period of several hours to get as complete a picture as possible of block activity within the data buffer.

Now that we understand how to monitor and tune the data buffer pools, let's return to a more general consideration of large blocks and their behavior in Oracle.

Large Blocks and Oracle Indexes

When an SQL query retrieves a result set from an Oracle table, it is probably gathering the table rows through an index. Many Oracle tuning experts have recommended that databases created prior to Oracle9i be re-defined with large block sizes. The performance gains realized from switching a 2K block size database to an 8K block size have perplexed many.

Resistance to increasing the block size was typically expressed as "Why will moving to a large block size improve a database that only randomly fetches small rows"? The answer to this question is not so simple, but it involves indexes.

Many DBAs fail to consider index trees and the index range scan process of sequential retrieval of the index when choosing a block size. Nested loop joins usually evidence an index range scan, and the vast majority of rows are accessed using indexes.

Locating indexes in larger size blocks reduces I/O and further improves throughput for the entire database because index range scans gather index nodes sequentially. If this is the case, why not just create the database with large block sizes and forget about multiple block sizes?

The answer here is also complex. RAM buffer memory cannot be utilized with maximum efficiency unless the tables are segregated according to the distribution of related data between them. In allocating block sizes, we can still apply the same general rules, with some modification in our understanding.

Small block size

Tables containing small rows that are accessed randomly should be placed into tablespaces with smaller block sizes. This way, more of the buffer RAM remains available to store rows from other tables that are referenced frequently.

Larger block size

Larger block sizes are suitable for indexes, row-ordered tables, single-table clusters, and tables with frequent full-table scans. In this way, a single I/O will retrieve many related rows, and future requests for related rows will already be available in the data buffer.

Some objects that may benefit from a larger blocksize (16K or 32K) include:

- Most indexes (because of the serial nature of index range scans)

- Large tables that are the target of full table scans

- Tables with large object (BLOB, CLOB, etc.) data

- Tables with large row sizes that might blossom into chained/migrated rows

- Temporary tablespaces used for sorting

The simple goal is to maximize the amount of RAM available to the data buffers by setting the block size according to the amount of I/O the table or index sees. Smaller block sizes are appropriate for randomly accessed small rows, while larger blocks are more suitable for rows sequentially accessed.

To illustrate, suppose a query retrieves 100 random 80 byte rows from Oracle. Since the rows are randomly accessed, we can safely assume that no two rows exist on the same block, implying that it is necessary to read 100 blocks to fulfill the task.

If the blocks are sized 16K, the *db_16k_cache_size* buffer will need 16 MB (16K * 100) of RAM. If the blocks are instead 2K, we only need 2 MB of RAM in the buffer for the 100 I/Os. Using the smaller block size would save 14 MB of RAM for this query alone, RAM that will be available elsewhere to hold other data.

Maximizing Oracle9i Block Space Usage

We will have to manage the RAM that is allocated to the data buffers until memory becomes cheap enough to cache the entire database. Properly allocating tables and indexes according to block size is a balancing act. If the data blocks are set too large, valuable buffer space is wasted holding row data that will never be referenced. If the blocks are set too small, Oracle is forced to perform more disk I/O to satisfy a query.

Here are some further general guidelines for allocating data block sizes:

- **Segregate large-table full-table scans** – Tables subject to large-table, full-table scans will benefit from the largest supported block size. They should be placed in a tablespace with the largest block size.

- **Set db_recycle_cache_size carefully** – If *db_cache_size* is not set to the largest supported block size, do not use the *db_recycle_cache_size* parameter. Instead, create a *db_32k_cache_size* (or whatever the max is), and assign all tables and indexes subject to large-table, full-table scans to the largest data buffer in the database.

Bear in mind that the data dictionary will use the default block size. Make sure that the dictionary (e.g. the SYSTEM tablespace) is always fully cached in a data buffer pool. The block size, per se, of the dictionary is less important than having enough RAM in the SYSTEM tablespace buffer to fully cache all of the dictionary blocks.

Summary of Block Size Rules

By now, you should be well aware of the importance of multiple block sizes and multiple RAM caches. Understanding the salient issues surrounding block sizes enables the DBA to intelligently assign block sizes to tables and indexes.

However, the DBA should also realize that tuning changes are never permanent, and he can experiment with different block sizes and with moving tables from one tablespace to another. For example, if the I/O increases after a table is moved into a 2K tablespace, it can simply be moved into a larger-sized tablespace. In the final analysis, minimizing I/O by adjusting block sizes is a long, iterative process.

The list below is a summary of rules for sizing objects into tablespaces of multiple block sizes:

- **Indexes want large block sizes** – B-tree indexes perform best in the largest supported block size. All indexes should reside in 32K block size tablespaces. This facilitates retrieval of as many index nodes as possible with a single I/O, especially for SQL performing index range scans.

- **Use average row length** – A tablespace should always have a larger block size than the average row length of the tables that reside in the tablespace (*avg_row_len* in the *dba_tables* view). Excessive I/O is incurred when the block size is smaller than the average row length due to row chaining.

- **Use large blocks for data sorting** – The TEMP tablespace will also benefit from the largest supported block size. Large blocks allow disk sorting with a minimum of disk I/O.

The introduction of Oracle9i has laid a foundation for a truly self-tuning data cache. It is only a matter of time before the database itself will dynamically change the buffer cache sizes in response to the needs of the application. For the time being however, the DBA must apply his intelligence to appropriately place tables and indexes into tablespaces that are optimally sized in order to reduce disk I/O.

Conclusion

The supplied information can be very useful for determining the data tables that are receiving the most I/O activity. This chapter has discussed techniques and provided valuable tools and scripts for monitoring and self-tuning the Oracle9i data buffers. Two of the salient points in the chapter are summarized below.

- The data buffer hit ratio can be monitored over long time periods using STATSPACK. Discovered trends and averages can be used to identify buffers that will benefit from RAM reconfiguration.

- The *v$sql_plan* view can be used to extract SQL execution plans and to find candidates for the KEEP and RECYCLE pools.

The next chapter will consider techniques for proactively reconfiguring the SGA.

Chapter 4

Proactive SGA Reconfiguration

There are three main areas that affect your decision to resize the Oracle RAM regions. While this book has been devoted to advanced scripts for detecting specific Oracle resource problems, all SGA self-tuning is generally done in one of these areas:

- *shared_pool_size* - A high value for any of the library cache miss ratios may signal the need to allocate more memory to the shared pool.

- *db_cache_size* - You may want to add RAM to the data buffer cache when the data buffer hit ratio falls below a predefined threshold.

- *pga_aggregate_target* - When you see high values for multi-pass executions, you may want to increase the available PGA memory.

Let's take a close look at each of these conditions.

Rules for adjusting *shared_pool_size*

We all know from Oracle8 that there are several queries for determining when the Oracle shared pool is too small. The library cache miss ratio tells the DBA whether to add space to the shared pool, and it represents the ratio of the sum of library cache reloads to the sum of pins.

In general, if the library cache ratio is over 1, you should consider adding to the *shared_pool_size*. Library cache misses occur during the parsing and preparation of the execution plans for SQL statements.

The compilation of an SQL statement consists of two phases: the parse phase and the execute phase. When the time comes to parse an SQL statement, Oracle checks to see if the parsed representation of the statement already exists in the library cache. If not, Oracle will allocate a shared SQL area within the library cache and then parse the SQL statement. At execution time, Oracle checks to see if a parsed representation of the SQL statement already exists in the library cache. If not, Oracle will reparse and execute the statement.

The following STATSPACK script will compute the library cache miss ratio. Note that the script sums all of the values for the individual components within the library cache and provides an instance-wide view of the health of the library cache.

---
rpt_lib_miss.sql

```
set lines 80;
set pages 999;

column mydate heading 'Yr.  Mo Dy  Hr.' format a16
column c1 heading "execs"     format 9,999,999
column c2 heading "Cache Misses|While Executing"     format
9,999,999
column c3 heading "Library Cache|Miss Ratio"     format 999.99999

break on mydate skip 2;

select
   to_char(snap_time,'yyyy-mm-dd HH24')   mydate,
   sum(new.pins-old.pins)                 c1,
   sum(new.reloads-old.reloads)           c2,
   sum(new.reloads-old.reloads)/
   sum(new.pins-old.pins)                 library_cache_miss_ratio
from
   stats$librarycache old,
   stats$librarycache new,
   stats$snapshot     sn
where
```

```
   new.snap_id = sn.snap_id
and
   old.snap_id = new.snap_id-1
and
   old.namespace = new.namespace
group by
   to_char(snap_time,'yyyy-mm-dd HH24')
;
```

Here is the output. This report can easily be customized to alert the DBA when there are excessive executions or library cache misses.

```
                            Cache Misses   Library Cache
Yr.  Mo Dy  Hr.     execs While Executing   Miss Ratio
----------------  --------- --------------- -----------------------
2001-12-11 10       10,338         3                   .00029
2001-12-12 10      182,477       134                   .00073
2001-12-14 10      190,707       202                   .00106
2001-12-16 10        2,803        11                   .00392
```

Once this report identifies a time period where there may be a problem, STATSPACK provides the ability to run detailed reports to show the behavior of the objects within the library cache.

In the preceding example, you see a clear RAM shortage in the shared pool between 10:00 A.M. and 11:00 A.M. each day. In this case, you could dynamically reconfigure the shared pool with additional RAM memory from the *db_cache_size* during this period.

Rules for Adjusting pga_aggregate_target

You may want to dynamically change the *pga_aggregate_target* parameter when any one of the following conditions is true:

- Whenever the value of the *v$sysstat* statistic "estimated PGA memory for one-pass" exceeds *pga_aggregate_target*, you want to increase *pga_aggregate_target*.

- Whenever the value of the *v$sysstat* statistic "workarea executions – multipass" is greater than 1 percent, the database may benefit from additional RAM memory.

- It is possible to over-allocate PGA memory, and you may consider reducing the value of *pga_aggregate_target* whenever the value of the *v$sysstat* row "workarea executions—optimal" consistently measures 100 percent.

Rules for Adjusting the Data Buffer Sizes

The following STATSPACK report alerts the DBA when the data buffer hit ratio falls below the preset threshold. It is very useful for pinpointing those times when decision support-type queries are being run, since a large number of large-table, full-table scans may make the data buffer hit ratio drop. This script also reports on all three data buffers, including the KEEP and RECYCLE pools, and it can be customized to report on individual pools.

Remember, the KEEP pool should always have enough data blocks to cache all table rows, while the RECYCLE pool should get a very low buffer hit ratio, since it seldom re-reads data blocks. If the data buffer hit ratio is less than 90 percent, you may want to increase *db_cache_size* (*db_block_buffers* in Oracle8i and earlier).

```
*****************************************************************
When the data buffer hit ratio falls below 90%, you
should consider adding to the db_cache_size parameter
*****************************************************************

yr.  mo dy Hr.   Name     bhr
------------- --------  -----
2001-01-27 09 DEFAULT    45
2001-01-28 09 RECYCLE    41
2001-01-29 10 DEFAULT    36
2001-01-30 09 DEFAULT    28
2001-02-02 10 DEFAULT    83
2001-02-02 09 RECYCLE    81
2001-02-03 10 DEFAULT    69
2001-02-03 09 DEFAULT    69
```

Here, you will note those times when you might want to dynamically increase the value of the *db_cache_size* parameter. In the case of the preceding output, you could increase the *db_cache_size* each day between 8:00 A.M. and 10:00 A.M., stealing RAM memory from *pga_aggregate_target*.

The single most important new feature of Oracle9i is the ability to dynamically modify almost all of the Oracle parameters. This gives the Oracle professional the ability to dynamically reconfigure the Oracle instance while it is running, whether in reaction to a current performance problem or in anticipation of an impending performance problem.

Because everything within the SGA can now be modified dynamically, it is critical to the Oracle professional to understand how to monitor the Oracle database to learn to recognize trends and patterns with the system and proactively reconfigure the database in anticipation of regularly scheduled resource needs.

With respect to ongoing database tuning activities, the Oracle DBA generally looks at these three areas.

- **Normal scheduled re-configuration** – A bimodal instance that performs OLTP and DSS during regular hours will benefit from a scheduled task to re-configure the SGA and PGA.

- **Trend-based dynamic reconfiguration** – You can use STATSPACK to predict those times when the processing characteristics change and use the *dbms_job* package to fire ad-hoc SGA and PGA changes.

- **Reactive reconfiguration** – Just as Oracle9i dynamically re-distributes RAM memory for tasks within the *pga_aggregate_target* region, the Oracle DBA can write scripts that steal RAM from an under-utilized area and re-allocate these RAM pages to another RAM area.

Scheduling SGA Reconfiguration

One of the most common techniques for reconfiguring an Oracle instance is to use a shell script. To illustrate a simple example, consider a database that runs in online transaction-processing mode during the day and data warehouse mode at night. For this type of database, the Oracle DBA can schedule a job to reconfigure the instance to the most appropriate configuration for the type of processing that is being done.

Oracle professionals generally use two tools for scheduling a dynamic reconfiguration. The most common approach is to use a UNIX cron job in order to schedule a periodic reconfiguration, while some other Oracle professionals prefer to use the Oracle *dbms_job* utility. Both of these approaches allow the Oracle professional to schedule a reconfiguration.

In the example, below we see a UNIX script that can be used to reconfigure Oracle for decision support processing. One must note the important changes to the configuration in the *shared_pool*, *db_cache_size*, and *pga_aggregate_target* in order to accommodate data warehouse activity.

Here is a script to change Oracle into DSS-mode each evening at 6:00 PM

change_sga.ksh

```
#!/bin/ksh

# First, we must set the environment . . . .
ORACLE_SID=$1
export ORACLE_SID
ORACLE_HOME=`cat /etc/oratab|grep ^$ORACLE_SID:|cut -f2 -d':'`
#ORACLE_HOME=`cat /var/opt/oracle/oratab|grep ^$ORACLE_SID:|cut -f2
-d':'`
export ORACLE_HOME
PATH=$ORACLE_HOME/bin:$PATH
export PATH

$ORACLE_HOME/bin/sqlplus -s /nologin<<!
connect system/manager as sysdba;
alter system set db_cache_size=1500m;
alter system set shared_pool_size=500m;
alter system set pga_aggregate_target=4000m;
exit
!
```

As we can see, writing scripts to re-configure the SGA is easy. Next, let's look at how to use buffer trend reports from Oracle STATSPACK to predict those times when the data buffers need additional RAM.

Trend-based Oracle Reconfiguration

A common approach to trend-based reconfiguration is to use STATSPACK historical data to proactively reconfigure the database. A good analogy is just-in-time manufacturing, where parts appear on the plant floor just as they are needed for assembly. Oracle9i enables the DBA to anticipate processing needs and regularly schedule appropriate intervention, insuring that SGA resources are delivered just-in-time for processing tasks.

For those who would like to investigate STATSPACK features and abilities at a deeper level, two informative books are available from Oracle Press:

- ***Oracle High-performance Tuning with STATSPACK*** - Oracle Press, by Donald K. Burleson.

- ***Oracle9i High-performance Tuning with STATSPACK*** - Oracle Press, by Donald K. Burleson.

The entire range of techniques and options available for trend identification using STATSPACK are beyond the scope of this book. We will concentrate here on examining STATSPACK reports that indicate trends in the behavior of the data buffer pools. Average data buffer hit ratios can be generated along two dimensions:

- Average DBHR by day of the week
- Average DBHR by hour of the day

Either of these reports will supply invaluable information for spotting usage trends in the Oracle database. Change occurs in the data buffers rapidly, and sometimes a long-term analysis will provide clues that point to processing problems within the database. Almost every Oracle database exhibits patterns that are linked to regular processing schedules, called signatures. The following sections will plot the average data buffer hit ratio for an Oracle database over different intervals.

Plotting the Data Buffer Hit Ratio by Hour of the Day

STATSPACK can easily compute the average DBHR by the hour of the day. Let's look closely at the script that performs this function, and notice that it references the *stats$buffer_pool_statistics* table. This table contains the values used for computing the DBHR. These values are time-specific, only indicative of conditions at the time of the STATSPACK snapshot. However, we need a technique that will yield an elapsed-time measure of the hit ratio.

To convert the values into elapsed-time data, we can join the *stats$buffer_pool_statistics* table against itself, and compare the original snapshot with each successive one. Since the desired collection interval is hourly, the script presented below will compute each hourly buffer hit ratio. We can further derive the hourly DBHR for each day by selecting the *snap_time* column with a mask of HH24.

rpt_bhr8i_hr.sql

```
-- ****************************************************************
-- Display hourly BHR averages with STATSPACK
--
-- Copyright (c) 2003 By Donald K. Burleson - All Rights reserved.
-- ****************************************************************

set pages 999;

column bhr format 9.99
column mydate heading 'yr.  mo dy Hr.'
select
   to_char(snap_time,'HH24')        mydate,
   avg(
   (((new.consistent_gets-old.consistent_gets)+
   (new.db_block_gets-old.db_block_gets))-
   (new.physical_reads-old.physical_reads))
   /
   ((new.consistent_gets-old.consistent_gets)+
   (new.db_block_gets-old.db_block_gets))
   ) bhr
```

```
from
   perfstat.stats$buffer_pool_statistics old,
   perfstat.stats$buffer_pool_statistics new,
   perfstat.stats$snapshot               sn
where
   new.name in ('DEFAULT','FAKE VIEW')
and
   new.name = old.name
and
   new.snap_id = sn.snap_id
and
   old.snap_id = sn.snap_id-1
and
   new.consistent_gets > 0
and
   old.consistent_gets > 0
having
   avg(
   (((new.consistent_gets-old.consistent_gets)+
   (new.db_block_gets-old.db_block_gets))-
   (new.physical_reads-old.physical_reads))
   /
   ((new.consistent_gets-old.consistent_gets)+
   (new.db_block_gets-old.db_block_gets))
   ) < 1
group by
   to_char(snap_time,'HH24')
;
```

CAUTION - A problem will arise with this script if the instance is stopped and restarted because the $v\$$ view values will be reset. STATSPACK will take a value from the previous instance when the database is restarted, invariably causing the utility to return an arbitrarily large number. We can circumvent this problem by adding the HAVING clause to the script, which omits any values greater than 1.

The output from the DBHR hourly average script is shown below. The report displays the average hit ratio for each day. The report provides insight, but the signature of the database becomes much more obvious if it is plotted in a spreadsheet.

```
yr    BHR
--    -----
00    .94
01    .96
02    .91
03    .82
04    .80
05    .90
06    .94
07    .93
08    .96
09    .95
10    .84
12    .91
13    .96
14    .95
17    .97
18    .97
19    .95
20    .95
21    .99
22    .93
23    .94
```

Oracle professionals use STATSPACK to extract the signatures for all of the important metrics and then plot the metrics to reveal the trend-based patterns. The signatures are typically gathered by hour of the day and day of the week.

A plot of the data is shown in Figure 4.1. Signatures become more evident over longer periods of time. Nevertheless, the plot of this database already evidences some interesting trends.

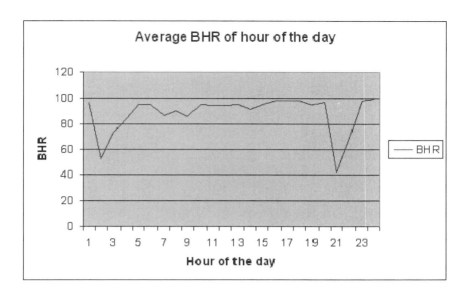

Figure 4.1 – A plot of buffer hit ratio averages by hour of day

It is immediately clear from the chart that the DBHR dropped below 90 percent at 3:00 a.m., 4:00 a.m. and 10:00 a.m. each day. In this case, end users of the database were submitting huge batch reports between 3:00 and 5:00 a.m. The difficulty for the DBA is that the 10:00 a.m. drop is a prime-time online period. To solve this problem, the DBA might review the SQL statements collected in the *stats$sql_summary* for the 9:00 to 10:00 a.m. periods to see if any rows have large *rows_processed* values. If so, the task could be rescheduled during off-peak processing hours.

Plotting the Data Buffer Hit Ratio by Day of the Week

A similar analysis will yield the average DBHR by day of the week. We only need change the script *snap_time* format mask from "HH24" to "day".

rpt_bhr8i_dy.sql

```
-- ***************************************************************
-- Display daily BHR averages with STATSPACK
--
-- Copyright (c) 2003 By Donald K. Burleson - All Rights reserved.
-- ***************************************************************

set pages 999;

column bhr format 9.99
column mydate heading 'yr.  mo dy Hr.'

select
   to_char(snap_time,'day')       mydate,
   avg(
   (((new.consistent_gets-old.consistent_gets)+
   (new.db_block_gets-old.db_block_gets))-
   (new.physical_reads-old.physical_reads))
   /
   ((new.consistent_gets-old.consistent_gets)+
   (new.db_block_gets-old.db_block_gets))
   ) bhr
from
   perfstat.stats$buffer_pool_statistics old,
   perfstat.stats$buffer_pool_statistics new,
   perfstat.stats$snapshot               sn
where
   new.name in ('DEFAULT','FAKE VIEW')
and
   new.name = old.name
and
   new.snap_id = sn.snap_id
and
   old.snap_id = sn.snap_id-1
and
   new.consistent_gets > 0
and
   old.consistent_gets > 0
having
   avg(
   (((new.consistent_gets-old.consistent_gets)+
   (new.db_block_gets-old.db_block_gets))-
   (new.physical_reads-old.physical_reads))
   /
   ((new.consistent_gets-old.consistent_gets)+
   (new.db_block_gets-old.db_block_gets))
   ) < 1
group by
   to_char(snap_time,'day')
;
```

The output from the script is below. Note that the days must be manually re-sequenced because they are given in

---

Creating a Self-Tuning Oracle Database

alphabetical order. This can be done after pasting the output into a spreadsheet for graphing.

```
yr.   mo d     BHR
--------- -----
friday        .89
monday        .98
saturday      .92
sunday        .91
thursday      .96
tuesday       .93
wednesday     .91
```

The resulting graph is shown in Figure 4.2.

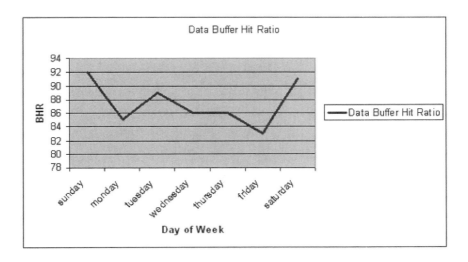

Figure 4.2 – Average data buffer hit ratio by day of the week

The graph clearly shows the need to increase the *db_cache_size* on Mondays and Fridays.

This report is useful in ascertaining a periodic or regular buffer signature. The DBHR of this database drops on Wednesdays and Fridays. To understand why, we would use STATSPACK to investigate the differences between these days and other days of the week.

This is all we need to know to plot and interpret data buffer hit ratios. We should also understand the value of trend analysis for indicating pattern signatures. Let's move on and look at some more STATSPACK script for tuning the structure of the SGA.

A script similar to the preceding DBHR scripts, but applied to the library cache, can reveal deficiencies within the shared pool. The utility takes time-based Oracle tuning information, such as the library cache miss ratio, and places it within Oracle tables.

Once we are familiar with the structure of the tables and columns within these tables, we can write simple Oracle queries that will display trend-based information. The trend-based data can then be applied to predictive models that inform the administrator of the appropriate times to change the internal structure of the SGA.

rpt_lib_cache_hr.sql

```
-- ****************************************************************
-- Display hourly library cache stats with STATSPACK
--
-- Copyright (c) 2003 By Donald K. Burleson - All Rights reserved.
-- ****************************************************************

set lines 80;
set pages 999;

column mydate heading 'Yr.  Mo Dy  Hr.'      format a16
column c1       heading "execs"               format 9,999,999
column c2       heading "Cache Misses|While Executing" format
9,999,999
column c3       heading "Library Cache|Miss Ratio" format 999.99999

break on mydate skip 2;

select
   to_char(snap_time,'yyyy-mm-dd HH24')  mydate,
   sum(new.pins-old.pins)                c1,
   sum(new.reloads-old.reloads)          c2,
   sum(new.reloads-old.reloads)/
   sum(new.pins-old.pins)                library_cache_miss_ratio
```

```
from
    stats$librarycache old,
    stats$librarycache new,
    stats$snapshot       sn
where
    new.snap_id = sn.snap_id
and
    old.snap_id = new.snap_id-1
and
    old.namespace = new.namespace
group by
    to_char(snap_time,'yyyy-mm-dd HH24');
```

The output below indicates a RAM shortage in the shared pool between 9:00 and 10:00 a.m.

			Cache Misses	Library Cache
Yr. Mo Dy	Hr.	execs	While Executing	Miss Ratio
2001-12-11	10	10,338	6,443	.64
2001-12-12	10	182,477	88,136	.43
2001-12-14	10	190,707	101,832	.56
2001-12-16	10	72,803	45,932	.62

The DBA merely needs to schedule additional RAM for the *shared_pool_size* during the deficient period (cron or *dbms_job*).

We know from the example above that a high amount of library cache meshes indicate that the shared pool is too small. To further summarize, a data buffer hit ratio of less than 90 percent for any of the seven Oracle data buffer pools indicates that memory should be moved from other database regions and reallocated to the data buffer area. Also, whenever the percentage of optimal executions within the PGA is less than 95, the value of the PGA aggregate target parameter should be increased.

Next let's examine those times that we should trigger a dynamic reconfiguration of Oracle.

When to Trigger a Dynamic Reconfiguration

The DBA must choose which RAM region to borrow memory from whenever the scripts indicate an overstressed RAM region. Table 4.1 displays the threshold condition for triggering a dynamic memory change.

RAM area	Overstressed Condition	Over-allocated Condition
Shared pool	Library cache misses	No misses
Data buffer cache	Hit ratio < 90%	Hit ratio > 95%
PGA aggregate	High multi-pass exec	100% optimal executions

Table 4.1 - Threshold Conditions for Dynamic RAM Reallocation

It is easy to schedule tasks that change the RAM memory configuration as the processing needs change on a UNIX platform. For example, it is common for Oracle databases to operate in OLTP mode during normal work hours and to perform the database services memory-intensive batch reports at night. We have noted that an OLTP database needs a large *db_cache_size* value. Memory-intensive batch tasks require additional RAM in the *pga_aggregate_target* parameter.

The UNIX scripts given below can be used to reconfigure the SGA between the OLTP and DSS without stopping the instance. The example assumes an isolated Oracle server with 8 gigabytes of RAM, with 10 percent of RAM reserved for UNIX overhead, leaving 7.2 gigabytes for Oracle and Oracle connections. The scripts are intended either for HP-UX or Solaris and accept the $ORACLE_SID as an argument.

This *dss_config.ksh* script will be run at 6:00 p.m. each evening in order to reconfigure Oracle for the memory-intensive batch tasks.

dss_config.ksh

```ksh
#!/bin/ksh

# First, we must set the environment . . . .
ORACLE_SID=$1
export ORACLE_SID
ORACLE_HOME=`cat /etc/oratab|grep ^$ORACLE_SID:|cut -f2 -d':'`
#ORACLE_HOME=`cat /var/opt/oracle/oratab|grep ^$ORACLE_SID:|cut -f2
-d':'`
export ORACLE_HOME
PATH=$ORACLE_HOME/bin:$PATH
export PATH

$ORACLE_HOME/bin/sqlplus -s /nologin<<!
connect system/manager as sysdba;
alter system set db_cache_size=1500m;
alter system set shared_pool_size=500m;
alter system set pga_aggregate_target=4000m;
exit
!
```

The script below will be run at 6:00 a.m. each morning to reconfigure Oracle for the OLTP usage during the day.

oltp_config.ksh

```ksh
#!/bin/ksh

# First, we must set the environment . . . .
ORACLE_SID=$1
export ORACLE_SID
ORACLE_HOME=`cat /etc/oratab|grep ^$ORACLE_SID:|cut -f2 -d':'`
#ORACLE_HOME=`cat /var/opt/oracle/oratab|grep ^$ORACLE_SID:|cut -f2
-d':'`
export ORACLE_HOME
PATH=$ORACLE_HOME/bin:$PATH
export PATH

$ORACLE_HOME/bin/sqlplus -s /nologin<<!
connect system/manager as sysdba;

alter system set db_cache_size=4000m;
alter system set shared_pool_size=500m;
alter system set pga_aggregate_target=1500m;

exit
!
```

Note that the *dbms_job* package can also be used to schedule the reconfigurations.

It should now be clear that the administrator can develop mechanisms to constantly monitor the processing demands on the database and issue *alter system* commands to dynamically respond to these conditions.

Approaches to Self-tuning Oracle9i Databases

The Oracle administrator must adjust the RAM configuration according to the types of connections the database experiences. Generally, queries against the *v$* structures and STATSPACK will pinpoint those times when Oracle connections change their processing characteristics. There are three approaches to automated tuning:

- **Normal scheduled reconfiguration** - A bimodal instance that performs OLTP and DSS during regular hours will benefit from a scheduled task to reconfigure the SGA and PGA.

- **Trend-based dynamic reconfiguration** - You can use STATSPACK to predict those times when the processing characteristics change and use the *dbms_job* package to fire ad-hoc SGA and PGA changes.

- **Dynamic reconfiguration** - Just as Oracle9i dynamically redistributes RAM memory for tasks within the *pga_aggregate_target* region, the Oracle DBA can write scripts that take RAM from an under-utilized area and reallocate these RAM pages to another RAM area.

Now, let's wrap-up with a discussion about a more volatile parameter and see how Oracle may evolve to allow super-fast dynamic reconfiguration.

The Future of Oracle Self-tuning

As people get more sophisticated in their self-tuning endeavors, many more Oracle metrics may become self-tuning. For example, there are dozens of self-tuning parameters that are considered immutable that may be found to be changeable. As an example, let's consider the *optimizer_index_cost_adj* parameter.

Oracle Corporation has invested millions of dollars in making the cost-based SQL optimizer (CBO) one of the most sophisticated tools ever created. The job of the CBO is to always choose the most optimal execution plan for any SQL statements.

However, there are some things that the CBO cannot detect. The type of SQL statements, the speed of the disks, and the load on the CPUs all affect the "best" execution plan for an SQL statement. For example, the best execution plan at 4:00 AM, when 16 CPUs are idle, may be quite different from the same query at 3:00 PM, when the system is 90% utilized.

Despite the name "Oracle," the CBO is not psychic, and it can never know in advance the exact load on the system. Hence, the Oracle professional must adjust the CBO behavior, and most Oracle professionals adjust the CBO with two parameters: *optimizer_index_cost_adj* and *optimizer_index_caching*.

The parameter *optimizer_index_cost_adj* controls the CBOs propensity to favor index scans over full-table scans. As we shall see, in a dynamic system, the "ideal" value for *optimizer_index_cost_adj* may change radically in just a few minutes, as the type of SQL and load on the database changes.

Is it possible to query the Oracle environment and intelligently determine the optimal setting for *optimizer_index_cost_adj*? Let's examine the issue. The *optimizer_index_cost_adj* parameters default to a value of 100 and can range in value from 1 to 10,000. A value of 100 means that equal weight is given to index versus multi-block reads. In other words, *optimizer_index_cost_adj* can be thought of as a "how much do I like full-table scans?" parameter.

With a value of 100, the CBO likes full-table scans and index scans equally, and a number lower than 100 tells the CBO that index scans are faster than full-table scans. However, even with a super-low setting (*optimizer_index_cost_adj=1*), the CBO will still choose full-table scans against no-brainers, like tiny tables that reside on two blocks.

In sum, the *optimizer_index_cost_adj* parameter is a weight that can be applied to the relative cost of physical disk reads for two types of block access:

- A single-block read (i.e. index fetch by ROWID)

- A multi-block read (a full-table scan, OPQ, sorting)

Physical disk speed is an important factor in weighing these costs. As disk access speed increases, the costs of a full-table scan vs. single block reads can become negligible. For example, the new TMS RamSan-210 solid-state disk provides up to 100,000 I/Os per second, six times faster than traditional disk devices. In a solid-state disk environment, disk I/O is much faster, and multi-block reads are far cheaper than traditional disks.

The speed of performing a full-table (SOFTS) scan depends on many factors:

- The number of CPUs on the system
- The setting for Oracle Parallel query (parallel hints, alter table)
- Table partitioning
- The speed of the disk I/O sub-system (e.g. hardware cached I/O, solid-state disk RAM-Disk)

With all of these factors, it may be impossible to determine the exact best setting for the weight in *optimizer_index_cost_adj*. In the real world, the decision to invoke a full-table scan is heavily influenced by run-time factors such as:

- The availability of free blocks in the data buffers
- The amount of TEMP tablespace (if the FTS has an *order by* clause)
- The current demands on the CPUs

Hence, it follows that the *optimizer_index_cost_adj* should be changing frequently, as the load changes on the server.

However, is it safe to assume that all of the SOFTS factors are reflected in the relative I/O speed of FTS versus index access? If we make this assumption, we have to measure the relative speed in *v$system_event* and have a foundation for creating a self-tuning parameter. To do this, we must accept several assumptions.

No systems are alike, and a good DBA must adjust *optimizer_index_cost_adj* according to the configuration and data access patterns. The SOFTS is measurable, and it is reflected in the wait times in *v$system_event*.

The overall amount of time spent performing full-table scans is equal to the percentage of 'db file sequential read' waits as a percentage of total I/O waits from *v$system_event*.

Here is a script that interrogates the *v$system_event* view and displays a suggested starting value for *optimizer_index_cost_adj*.

---

optimizer_index_cost_adj.sql

```
col c1 heading 'Average Waits for|Full Scan Read I/O'      format 9999.999
col c2 heading 'Average Waits for|Index Read I/O'          format 9999.999
col c3 heading 'Percent of| I/O Waits|for Full Scans'      format 9.99
col c4 heading 'Percent of| I/O Waits|for Index Scans'     format 9.99
col c5 heading 'Starting|Value|for|optimizer|index|cost|adj' format 999

select
   a.average_wait                                   c1,
   b.average_wait                                   c2,
   a.total_waits /(a.total_waits + b.total_waits)   c3,
   b.total_waits /(a.total_waits + b.total_waits)   c4,
   (b.average_wait / a.average_wait)*100            c5
from
   v$system_event   a,
   v$system_event   b
where
   a.event = 'db file scattered read'
and
   b.event = 'db file sequential read'
;
```

Here is the listing from this script:

Average Waits for Full Scan Read I/O	Average Waits for Index Read I/O	Percent of I/O Waits for Full Scans	Percent of I/O Waits for Index Scans	Starting Value for optimizer index cost adj
1.473	.289	.02	.98	20

As you can see, the suggested starting value for *optimizer_index_cost_adj* may be too high because 98% of data waits are on index (sequential) block access. How can we "weight" this starting value for *optimizer_index_cost_adj* to reflect the reality that this system has only 2% waits on full-table scan reads (a typical OLTP system with few full-table scans)? As a practical matter, we never want an automated value for *optimizer_index_cost_adj* to be less than 1, nor more than 100.

Also, these values change constantly. As the I/O waits accumulate and access patterns change, this same script may give a very different result at a different time of the day.

Average Waits for Full Scan Read I/O	Average Waits for Index Read I/O	Percent of I/O Waits for Full Scans	Percent of I/O Waits for Index Scans	Starting Value for optimizer index cost adj
1208.249	212.676	.08	.92	18

This example has served to show the dynamic nature of an active database and demonstrate the value of being able to dynamically change important parameters as the processing load on the system changes.

Book Conclusion

Tuning the database can become quite complex, but Oracle9i offers the administrator an unparalleled ability to control the PGA and SGA. Until Oracle9i evolves into a completely self-tuning architecture, the DBA will be responsible for adjusting the dynamic configuration of the system RAM.

This short book is intended to give the DBA a high-level overview of the salient features involved in scheduling dynamic reconfigurations within Oracle. In the future, we may expect complete self-tuning databases to emerge, but in the meantime, the administrator must track the historical behavior of the database and apply it to predictive models. It is only in this way that scarce instance resources can be proactively applied to develop an optimally-tuned Oracle database.

As an Oracle author, I am always happy to hear from my readers. If you have any comments, suggestions, or enhancements that you have made to these scripts, please feel free to e-mail me at don@burleson.cc.

Also, for ongoing Oracle tips and Oracle information, please visit my web site at www.dba-oracle.com.

Best Regards,

Don Burleson

Index

The Oracle In-Focus™ Series

The *Oracle In-Focus*™ series is a unique publishing paradigm, targeted at Oracle professionals who need fast and accurate working examples of complex issues. *Oracle In-Focus*™ books are unique because they have a super-tight focus and quickly provide Oracle professionals with what they need to solve their problems.

Oracle In-Focus™ books are designed for the practicing Oracle professional. Oracle In-Focus™ books are an affordable way for all Oracle professionals to get the information they need, and get it fast.

- **Expert Authors** – All *Oracle In-Focus*™ authors are content experts and are carefully screened for technical ability and communications skills.

- **Online Code Depot** – All code scripts from *Oracle In-Focus*™ are available on the web for instant download. Those who purchase a book will get the URL and password to download their scripts.

- **Lots of working examples** – *Oracle In-Focus*™ is packed with working examples and pragmatic tips.

- **No theory** – Practicing Oracle professionals know the concepts, they need working code to get started fast.

- **Concise** – All *Oracle In-Focus*™ books are less than 200 pages and get right to-the-point of the tough technical issues.

- **Tight focus** - The *Oracle In-Focus*™ series addresses tight topics and targets specific technical areas of Oracle technology.

- **Affordable** – Reasonably priced, *Oracle In-Focus*™ books are the perfect solution to challenging technical issues.

http://www.rampant.cc/

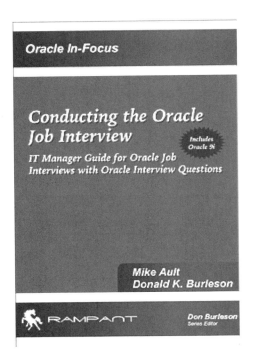

Conducting the Oracle Job Interview

IT Manager's Guide for Oracle Job Interviews with Oracle Interview Questions

Mike Ault & Don Burleson
ISBN 0-9727513-1-9
Publication Date – Feb 2003
Retail Price $16.95 / £10.95

As professional consultants, Don Burleson and Mike Ault have interviewed hundreds of Oracle job candidates. With over four decades of interviewing experience, Ault and Burleson tell you how to quickly identify acceptable Oracle job candidates by asking the right Oracle job interview questions.

Mike Ault and Don Burleson are recognized as the two best-selling Oracle Authors in the world. With combined authorship of over 25 books, Ault & Burleson are the two most respected Oracle authorities on the planet. For the first time ever, Ault & Burleson combine their talents in this exceptional handbook.

Using Oracle job interview questions that are not available to the general public, the IT manager will be able to quickly access the technical ability of any Oracle job candidate. In today's market, there are thousands of under-trained Oracle professionals, and the IT manager must be able to quickly access the true ability of the Oracle job candidate.

http://www.rampant.cc/

Oracle9i RAC

Oracle Real Application Clusters Configuration and Internals

Mike Ault & Madhu Tumma
ISBN 0-9727513-0-0
Publication Date - June 2003
Retail Price $59.95 / £37.95

Combining the expertise of two world-renowned RAC experts, Oracle9i RAC is the first-of-its-find reference for RAC and TAF technology. Learn from the experts how to quickly optimizer your Oracle clustered server environment for optimal performance and flexibility.

Covering all areas of RAC continuous availability and transparent application failover, this book is indispensable for any Oracle DBA who is charged with configuring and implementing a RAC clusters database.

Mike Ault is one of the world's most famous Oracle authors with 14 books in-print, and Madhu Tumma is a recognized RAC clustering consultant. Together, Ault and Tumma dive deep inside RAC and show you the secrets for quickly implementing and tuning Oracle9i RAC database systems.

http://www.rampant.cc/

Oracle Utilities

Using Hidden Programs, Import/Export, SQL*Loader, oradebug, Dbverify, Tkprof and More

Dave Moore
ISBN 0-9727513-5-1
Publication Date - June 2003
Retail Price $27.95 / £17.95

Written by one of the world's top DBAs and architect of the famous DBXray(tm) product by BMC Software, Dave Moore targets his substantial knowledge of Oracle internals at the Oracle supplied utilities. Intended for Senior Oracle professionals, these powerful utilities are hidden deep inside Oracle and Dave Moore can show you how to unleash the hidden power of these Oracle utilities.

Deep inside the operating system executables there are many utilities are at the fingertips of Oracle professionals, but until now, there has been no advice on how to use these utilities. From tnsping.exe to dbv.exe to wrap.exe, Dave Moore describes each utility and has working examples in the online code depot. Your timesaving from a single script is worth the price of this great book.

http://www.rampant.cc/

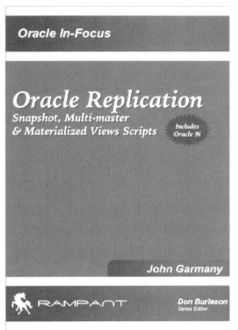

Oracle Replication

Snapshot, Multi-master &
Materialized Views Scripts

John Garmany
ISBN 0-9727513-3-5
Publication Date - Dec 2003
Retail Price $27.95 / £17.95

This book is an indispensable reference for any Oracle DBA who must ensure the consistency of data across distributed platforms. With the advent of cheap disk and fast worldwide connectivity, many Oracle professionals recognize the benefits of distributing Oracle data. However, Oracle multi-master replication is extremely complex and time-consuming to implant. This book addresses the complexity of Oracle replication by providing working code examples and illustration from working systems. The text covers all areas of Oracle replication, including snapshots, using dbms_job to refresh snapshots, multi-master replication and conflict resolution mechanisms.

Written by a distinguished graduate of West Point, Col. Garmany leverages his 20+ years of experience into an indispensable guide for any Oracle professional who must quickly implement Oracle snapshot and multimaster replication. A noted instructor, author and lecturer, Col. John Garmany leverages his ability to explain complex issues in Plain English into a one-of-a-kind book.

http://www.rampant.cc/

Oracle High-Performance SQL Tuning

Donald Burleson
Publisher: McGraw-Hill
Osborne Media; 1st edition
(July 27, 2001)
ISBN: 0072190582
Copyright: 2001
Retail Price $49.99 US

From the official Oracle Press comes a comprehensive guide to tuning SQL statements for optimal execution. This expert resource explains how to view the internal execution plan of any SQL statement and change it to improve the performance of the statement. You'll get details on Oracle's optimizer modes, SQL extensions, the STATSPACK utility, and a wealth of methods for tuning Oracle SQL statements.

Tune all types of SQL statements--from a simple SELECT statement to a complex non-correlated subquery--using tips and techniques from SQL expert Don Burleson. Officially authorized by Oracle Corporation, this in-depth resource explains how to take any SQL statement, view the internal execution plan, and change the execution plan to improve the performance of the statement. You'll get details on Oracle's optimizer modes, SQL extensions, the STATSPACK utility, and a wealth of methods for tuning Oracle SQL statements.

Oracle9i High-Performance Tuning with STATSPACK

Donald Burleson
Oracle Press, Feb 2002
Publisher: McGraw-Hill
Osborne Media;
March 22, 2002
ISBN: 007222360X
Copyright: 2001
Retail Price $49.99 US

Get complete coverage of STATSPACK--Oracle's powerful tuning tool--inside this official guide. Including ready-to-use STATSPACK scripts you'll be able to collect and analyze system data and soon have your Oracle database running at peak performance.

Burleson Oracle Consulting

Oracle Training – This is a popular option for Oracle shops who want a world-class Oracle instructor at reasonable rates. Burleson-designed courses are consistently top-rated, and we provide on-site Oracle training and Oracle classes at standards that exceed those of other Oracle education providers.

On-site Oracle consulting – Don Burleson is available to travel to your site for short-term Oracle support. Common on-site Oracle consulting support activities include short-term Oracle tuning, Oracle database troubleshooting, Oracle9i migration, Oracle design reviews and Oracle requirements evaluation support. Oracle support and Oracle consulting services are priced by the hour, so you only pay for what you need. These one-time Oracle consulting services commonly include:

- Answering questions from your Oracle DBA technical staff

- Repairing down production Oracle database systems

- One-time Oracle tuning

- Installation of Oracle application packages

Oracle Tuning – Don Burleson wrote the book on Oracle tuning and specializes in improving Oracle performance on Oracle8, Oracle8i and Oracle9i. His best-selling Oracle performance books include *High-Performance Oracle8 Tuning, Oracle High-Performance tuning with STATSPACK*, and *Oracle*

High-Performance SQL Tuning by Oracle Press. Don Burleson also specializes in Oracle SQL tuning.

Oracle Monitoring – As the author of the landmark book *Oracle High-Performance Tuning with STATSPACK*, Don Burleson offers a complete Oracle monitoring package, installed and tested on your server.

Oracle Project Management – Don Burleson provides complete Oracle design, starting from the initial concept all the way through implementation. Burleson has a proven history of designing robust and reliable Oracle database architectures and can recommend appropriate hardware, software, tools and Oracle support.

Oracle Data Warehouse Design & Implementation – As the author of *High-Performance Oracle Data Warehousing*, Burleson is often called upon to provide Oracle DBA support for Oracle8 data warehouse projects.

Oracle Design and Oracle Performance Reviews – This is great insurance before your Oracle database goes live. The review ensures that your application will be able to support production user volumes and that it will perform according to your specifications. Burleson is also expert at Oracle scalability, and he can conduct stress testing to ensure that your production database will be able to support high-volume transaction rates.

Oracle New Features Planning – This is a popular service where your specific needs are diagnosed and specific Oracle8i and Oracle9i features are identified for your database. We also provide upgrade services for Oracle applications, including 11i.

Oracle Applications Support - We offer world-class Oracle Applications support and offer the best rates for upgrading Oracle Applications, including 11i.

Remote Oracle DBA Support - BEI Remote DBA offers world-class remote Oracle support for companies that are too small to have a full-time Oracle DBA.

Burleson Oracle Consulting also has a vast network of Oracle consulting contacts and we can supply Oracle professionals for all Oracle projects, from short Oracle engagements to large-scale Oracle projects. BEI only employs consultants with extensive experience and knowledge.

Burleson Oracle Training

Burleson Oracle Training has been developing database training courses for 23 years. A former IT Professor, Donald Burleson has taught hundreds of Oracle Training classes and excels at developing Oracle training that explains complex computer topics in plain English. Don has developed customized Oracle training for some of the world's largest corporations.

Our most popular Oracle Training
Oracle Network Administration
> 4-Day on-site Oracle course - Oracle Training in Net8.

Oracle Administration & Management
> 5-Day on-site Oracle course - Oracle Training in Oracle Database administration and database management.

Getting started with Oracle SQL
> 3-Day on-site Oracle course - Hands-on Oracle training in SQL, SQL*Plus and SQL built-in functions.

- ## New Oracle9i Training
Oracle9i New Features
> A 3-Day on-site Oracle9i course - Oracle9i Training in all new features of Oracle9i

Advanced Oracle9i SQL Tuning
> 3-Day on-site Oracle course - Oracle training in all aspects of Oracle SQL tuning by the author of the best-selling

Oracle High-Performance SQL Tuning
by Oracle Press.

Oracle Training for Oracle Professionals

Oracle SQL and PL/SQL
5-Day on-site Oracle course - Hands-on Oracle Training in SQL, SQL*Plus and PL/SQL Oracle programming

Oracle Features, Administration & Tuning
2-Day on-site Oracle course - Oracle training for the DBA

Introduction to Oracle for End-users
5-Day on-site Oracle course - Hands-on Oracle Training.

For Corporate
Consulting & Training
Call Toll Free
866-729-8145